'This is a devastating critique of a political system in which the power of vested interests ensured that the state abrogated its duty to protect homeowners and tenants. Eoin Ó Broin details the human cost of the self-certification of building regulations that was in place until recent years and asks whether even now we have a regime fit for purpose.'

Mick Clifford

Eoin Ó Broin is a TD for Dublin Mid-West and Sinn Féin's spokesperson on Housing, Local Government and Heritage. He is the author of *Matxinada, Basque Nationalism and Radical Basque Youth Movements* (LRB 2003), *Sinn Féin and the Politics of Left Republicanism* (Pluto 2009) and *HOME: Why Public Housing is the Answer* (Merrion Press 2019). He writes regularly on housing policy issues for a range of newspapers and online publications.

DEFECTS

Living with the Legacy
of the Celtic Tiger

EOIN Ó BROIN

MERRION
PRESS

First published in 2021 by
Merrion Press
10 George's Street
Newbridge
Co. Kildare
Ireland
www.merrionpress.ie

9781785373961 (Paper)
9781785373985 (Epub)

A CIP catalogue record for this book is
available from the British Library.

Typeset in Sabon LT Std 11/15 pt

Cover designed by Fiachra McCarthy
www.fiachramccarthy.com
Back cover image © Alan Betson / THE IRISH TIMES

Merrion Press is a member of Publishing Ireland.

Thanks

To Lynn ... for everything.

To Ailbhe ... for continued advice, assistance and patience.

To Bóthar Buí (Sarah and Kieran) for another inspirational though sadly interrupted stay in January 2020.

To the BRegsBlog group for all the assistance since 2016.

To Deirdre Ní Fhloinn for corrections, comments and the important additional reading material.

Contents

Acknowledgements

To Paul Coleman, Paul Kavanagh and Sinead O'Flaherty for first bringing the issue of latent defects to my attention in 2013 and for having the courage to take a stand for what is right.

To Ciara Holland, Lorraine and Gary Carew, Mark, Aine and Alan, and Michael Doherty for being so open and honest with their experience of living with latent defects.

Particular thanks to Stephanie Meehan for demonstrating such bravery and generosity despite the enormous cost she and her children have had to pay for building defects they did not cause.

To all those journalists from local and national print and broadcast media who have continuously brought the issue of latent defects to light, exposed those responsible and given a voice to those most affected. Their work is important and must be continued.

To all involved in the Construction Defects Alliance for bringing owners together, coordinating their campaign and giving hope to so many people.

OVERTURE

An Unnecessary Death

On that morning, Stephanie woke later than usual. Her 7-year-old son Oisin hadn't been sleeping well, so she spent the night downstairs in the children's bedroom. As she opened her eyes and stretched to start the day, her partner Fiachra should have been up and out already, hard at work.

She looked out of the window and saw Fiachra's van in the driveway. 'That's strange,' she thought.

Stephanie picked up her phone and dialled, twice, but no answer. She shouted, 'Fiachra, you're late for work, you're late for work' as she climbed the stairs to the third floor.

When she opened the door to their bedroom, Fiachra was there. Stephanie touched his face. It was stone cold. He was dead. He had hanged himself during the night. It was Monday, 15 July 2013.

Thirty-eight-year-old Fiachra Daly was a hard-working family man. He loved his partner, Stephanie Meehan, and their two young children, Oisin and Cerys. He had a good job with DGM installing gas boilers. He worked long hours, often coming home well after 8 p.m. According to Stephanie, he was the kind of man who believed that 'you should get out of life what you put into it'. But since the problems had started to emerge in their apartment in Priory Hall some years earlier, Fiachra 'felt he wasn't getting what he should have gotten'.

Stephanie, Fiachra and their two children were among the 256 residents evacuated from their homes in the north Dublin development on foot of a court order in 2011. Priory Hall had significant fire-safety defects, and the developer, Tom McFeely, had failed to address the problems, despite a previous court ruling.

Fiachra and his family were placed in emergency accommodation, first in one hotel and then another, for several weeks. Then they were moved to a house owned by the National Asset Management Agency (NAMA) in nearby Belmayne.

Initially they had continued to pay their mortgage on the Priory Hall property. They were told that they would only be out of their home for a few weeks. But weeks turned into months and, out of anger and frustration, they stopped paying their lender, KBC.

In the months before his death, Fiachra was increasingly stressed. The bank would ring every single day. Then, when a moratorium was eventually agreed, there were the intrusive financial statements to be filled out.

While Stephanie threw herself into the residents' campaign at Priory Hall, attending meetings and vigils, Fiachra 'turned in on himself'.

'Looking back with hindsight,' Stephanie said, 'he wasn't dealing with it well.' He stopped going out, didn't want to socialise, even avoided family occasions.

Stephanie remembers Sunday, 14 July 2013 as a beautiful, sunny day. They were due to go to her mother's house for a barbecue, to take their mind off the stress of it all. Fiachra didn't want to go. Stephanie felt he needed a break from the kids.

When she got home, Fiachra was unusually anxious about a KBC financial statement request that had arrived during the week. While the bank had granted the moratorium on payments, they were still charging interest, and the letter said they owed an extra €20,000. He was angry. He worked hard, looked after his family, paid his taxes, did everything right. Why were his family being treated like this? Stephanie said he was 'really, really unhappy'.

The post-mortem returned an open verdict. The Dublin coroner Dr Brian Farrell said that because Fiachra had a high level of alcohol in his system, it was not possible to say whether he was in clear mind. His death may have been self-inflicted, but the coroner could not determine whether it had been intended.

Speaking to journalists after the inquest in August 2014, Stephanie said that Fiachra's death 'happened completely out of the blue. Everybody was very surprised. He was a very happy, kind person. Everyone was equally shocked.'[1]

Despite dealing with the grief of losing her partner, Stephanie had the strength to write to the then Taoiseach, Enda Kenny.

Dear Enda,

I have emailed you on many occasions, regarding my situation in Priory Hall. You have replied once.

On July 15th mine and my children's lives changed forever, my beautiful, kind, caring partner and father to my children took his own life. His name is Fiachra Daly. We miss him terribly. My life will never be the same. My children's lives will never be the same.

Fiachra was the happiest man on earth, he lived for myself, Oisin (7) and Cerys (2), he never suffered from any form of mental illness or depression, we had been together for 17 years and I never once witnessed any signs.

That is up until the week prior to his death, when we received demands from banks, looking for payment on arrears on a property that we can't live in, asking us to fill out, yet again, forms to request an extension of our moratorium, all for a property that we can't live in through no fault of our own. The stress, the worry of not being able to provide a safe home for us, his young children, eventually took its toll, as it has on every resident.

He was obviously a silent sufferer, he never complained, he supported me when I was feeling low, he hated the idea that he couldn't provide a safe home for us, that I do know, but I thought we'd battle through this together. How wrong was I?

I now have no home, my children have no permanent home but most importantly I have no partner and my children have lost their wonderful dad.

Our future, security and certainty changed the minute we were evacuated and not one thing has changed in two years, every email, phone call, letter seems to have fallen on deaf ears.

So, I ask you, what will it take for someone to listen and act on something that should have been dealt with two years ago and saved a lot of taxpayers money and most of all saved a life?

Tom McFeely walks around scot-free, he'll never suffer how we are suffering, he'll never lose what I've lost. He'll start again, I am left with a lifetime of heartache and my children will inherit that too.

Is there any justice in this country?

I've lost Fiachra, but I've not lost my voice.

Stephanie Meehan

For two years, residents from Priory Hall had been trying to secure a meeting with the government and, in particular, with the Minister for the Environment, Phil Hogan, whose remit included fire safety, building control, local government and housing. But time and again the minister refused to meet.

The official line was that enforcement of fire safety and building control were matters for Dublin City Council and legal enforcement was before the courts so the 'Minister and the Department must respect the independence of the designated statutory authority in these matters and cannot interfere in individual cases'.[2]

In November 2011, just a month after the evacuation of Priory Hall, opposition deputies Dessie Ellis (Sinn Féin) and Tommy Broughan (Labour), during a Dáil debate, called on

Hogan to meet with the residents and assist in securing a resolution. Read with hindsight, the government's response, particularly in light of Fiachra Daly's tragic death, is chilling:

> Residents at Priory Hall and their representatives have previously been advised … the appropriate statutory powers in this case rest with Dublin City Council and that neither the Minister nor the Department has a statutory function in enforcement activity or in determining the provision of services in individual cases. This is and will remain the position. While this may be of disappointment to the residents, it is important that the Minister act appropriately and within his powers, particularly in cases such as this which are already the subject of legal proceedings.[3]

While the initial response from the Taoiseach's office to Stephanie Meehan's heartfelt plea was muted, public pressure started to build. On 4 September, Enda Kenny gave a 'personal commitment to resolve the saga within the lifetime of the Government'.[4] In turn, Minister Phil Hogan relented and promised to meet the residents.

'What will it take for someone to act?' asked Stephanie Meehan. Unfortunately, it took the life of her partner Fiachra Daly to, in the words of an *Irish Times* editorial, 'galvanise action at the highest level'. The editorial rightly said, 'Remarkably, this knocking together of heads produced the terms of a settlement after three weeks of negotiations.'[5]

Within weeks of Fiachra's death, the stalled mediation process between the residents and banks concluded. The full deal was communicated to the residents during a meeting with Taoiseach Enda Kenny.

Owner-occupiers could walk away from their Priory Hall homes debt free and start again. Dublin City Council would acquire and refurbish the apartments within two years at an estimated cost of €10 million. Buy-to-let landlords would get a moratorium on their mortgages for the duration of the works. The implementation of the deal would be overseen by Dr Martin McAleese, the husband of President of Ireland Mary McAleese.

Speaking after the residents had accepted the deal, their spokesperson, Graham Usher, said that 'After a two-year battle the former occupants are looking forward to moving on with our lives and to paying our mortgages on new and safe homes, we can finally put Priory Hall behind us.'[6]

Usher singled out Stephanie for particular mention, saying that it was her 'strength and dignity that made this Government finally take notice of the national disgrace that is Priory Hall and brought them to act. The price Stephanie paid is more than anyone should have to, and every resident owes her a debt of gratitude.'[7]

For Stephanie, however, and Oisin and Cerys, they will never be able to put Priory Hall behind them. On the day the deal was agreed, Stephanie said, 'What I would wish for today is that Fiachra was here to celebrate this moving forward with me. This nightmare is over for all the residents but it's not over for me.'[8]

An *Irish Times* editorial written after the final deal was secured said, 'What galls those involved is the apparent determination of the Department of the Environment to evade any responsibility.' The paper's view was very clear: 'This disgraceful evasion must end.'[9]

But the question has to be asked, if the government had become involved earlier 'to galvanise action at the highest level', would the hardship experienced by the residents of Priory Hall have come to an end sooner and, crucially, would Fiachra Daly still be alive today?

Eight years have passed since Fiachra's untimely and unnecessary death. Stephanie has remarried and lives with her husband, Ritchie, and Oisin and Cerys in Clare Hall, just minutes away from Priory Hall. Oisin is 15 years old now and doing exams. Stephanie says he has great male role models around him with her father Michael, Ritchie and her brother Conleth, who lives nearby. But Oisin is still 'struggling with his father's death'. 'He has that extra burden, that extra baggage,' she says, and as a consequence suffers from post-traumatic stress disorder. Cerys is 10 years old, and while she was 'only 2 at the time, will still have problems', says Stephanie. 'She was the apple of her dad's eye.'

Dublin City Council have completed the refurbishment of the development, and families have started moving into their homes in what is now called New Priory.

Stephanie walks past it a lot. When asked how the development makes her feel, she said, 'It's only a building, I don't feel anything towards it.' She says she is glad it is being rebuilt and 'glad it will provide homes for people'. But she is still angry at those responsible for the trauma that her family and her neighbours were put through.

When asked how she feels when she hears the name Tom McFeely, her response is incredibly generous:

> I don't know, I don't really have any feelings about him to be honest. For years I wished him ill will and I didn't want him to have any luck in the world. Now I just kind of feel, you know, he can't be happy. He cannot be happy. He cannot close his eyes at night

and feel happy with how he has led his life. And if he is, if he feels okay about that then he's definitely not a normal human being. I don't wish him any harm. I know he's got children as well. So, I always felt that when people said, 'You must hate him', I don't hate him; I just think he's not a good person.

The one thing Stephanie is very clear about is that McFeely should never be allowed to build again. 'I would hope that he never gets a building licence,' she said. 'He doesn't deserve to build, he doesn't deserve to gain monetarily from building ... he should be struck off.'

The cost of rebuilding Priory Hall was €45 million. Providing emergency accommodation to the families forced from their homes cost a further €5 million. It is expected that up to €30 million will be recouped from the sale of the apartments at New Priory. The final net cost to the state will still be in the region of €20 million. But the human cost, particularly for Stephanie Meehan and her children, is immeasurable.

Neither Tom McFeely nor Laurence O'Mahony, his co-director at Coalport, the company that developed Priory Hall, ever went to jail for what they did. Instead, they filed for bankruptcy. Initially it looked like McFeely could be back in business by 2015, but following a High Court decision, the period was extended to 2020.

He exited bankruptcy on 30 March 2020, free to start building again. There is nothing in Irish law that prevents him from doing so.

PART 1

CHAPTER ONE

The Biggest Purchase of Your Life

'Absolutely over the moon'

Stephanie Meehan grew up in Baldoyle, five minutes from Priory Hall. She went to school locally, socialised in the area and ended up working in catering in the busy restaurant strip in Howth.

At the young age of 18 she met Fiachra Daly, who worked in the same cluster of restaurants in the picturesque seaside village. At first, they were friends. Three years later, they were in a relationship. She talks about socialising with work friends from the restaurant scene, of having a 'good life' with Fiachra filled with 'happy times'.

The couple were renting together in Howth. In 2005 their first child, Oisin, was born and they decided to move closer to Stephanie's family. They found a 'gorgeous apartment' in Grattan Lodge, right beside what was to become Priory Hall. Both were working hard and paying a hefty €915 rent per month. But they didn't care, they had Oisin, they had steady jobs and they had each other.

When Priory Hall came on the market, Stephanie said, 'We were very interested.' They assumed that the apartments would be the same as Grattan Lodge: spacious, with great views.

In May 2005 the *Irish Times* property section announced, 'Modern suburban apartments in D13'. The article went on to describe a 49 sq. m. one-bedroom showroom that had just opened, being sold through HOK Residential for €190,000. The two-bedroom apartments were 63 sq. m. and retailed at €240,000 to €249,000. The larger two-bedroom duplexes with 89 sq. m. were going for €288,000; the 3-bedroom 90 sq. m. duplexes, €290,000.

'Each unit is dual aspect', continued the article, 'and is fitted out to a high standard, with fitted wardrobes in all units and wall tiling in the main bathroom and en suite, chrome shower doors, decorative coving in hallways and sitting rooms and generous apartments.'

Stephanie and Fiachra were saving a lot for a deposit but found it very difficult to get a mortgage. 'We had a lot of refusals,' she remembers. Lenders took a dim view of the long-term security of restaurant work.

But with help from family and a friendly broker, they eventually secured a loan from IIB, now KBC. 'Everybody just wanted to see us get on the property ladder,' said Stephanie. And though they both knew that 'Priory Hall wasn't going to be their forever home', they felt good about getting a 'footstep to having our own house at some stage'.

When asked how she felt when she finally got the mortgage, Stephanie said, 'Absolutely over the moon. I was just thinking this is the start to a very secure and stable life.' She and Fiachra were 'setting out some foundations for our children and our family'. Indeed her 'whole family were relieved ... you just felt a great sense of security'.

'It was a sense of relief'

If you stand on one of the top balconies of Priory Hall and look east, you can see Belmayne. Built not long after its neighbour, it was an ambitious 2,650 home development just off the Malahide Road in north Dublin. The scheme was to include two schools, a medical centre, a library, a crèche, a town centre, a child-friendly park and a range of shops and bars. This wasn't just a development; it was a new suburb.

For 35-year-old Mark, Belmayne ticked a lot of boxes. Back living in his parents' home after years of renting, he was saving for a deposit. 'I was in a job that offered me access to credit for a property,' he said, and having 'spent quite a lot of time looking for somewhere to purchase', he finally settled on Belmayne.

Prices were at their Celtic Tiger height in 2007 and the flat he bought was 'far too expensive at €330,000 for a two bed'. But a lot of his friends had moved over to the northside of the city and 'generally properties were more competitively priced there'. The development was also 'quite well finished'.

Mark travelled a bit for work and, being close to Dublin Airport, Belmayne had the advantage of not being too far from the city centre while close to the terminal.

His idea was to 'get a first home'. He had a steady girlfriend and, though not yet married, wanted 'a starter home'. He remembers the day he moved in. 'I think I was the first one into the block,' he said. 'It was a sense of relief.' Despite the hefty mortgage, the first five years were interest only, so the young couple felt like they were doing well to be paying €600 per month.

Belmayne epitomised the Celtic Tiger brash self-image of wealth and glamour. And while Mark's decision to buy in the new suburb was determined by price and location, the developer, Stanley Holdings, were not just selling houses, they were selling lifestyles.

The construction site hoardings had high-definition photographs of glammed-up models with slogans like 'Gorgeous living comes to Dublin' and 'Afterhours @ Belmayne'. The not-so-subtle sexual undertones of the ads included a handsome young man dressed in black about to mount his model partner on the kitchen island with bottles of champagne placed conspicuously in the background.

The interiors of the showroom were designed by UK TV celebrity decorator Laurence Llewellyn-Bowen, while the gardens were by Irish celebrity landscaper Diarmuid Gavin. To add that extra bit of bling, the launch party was attended by the celebrity soccer and pop-star couple Jamie and Louise Redknapp.

If Mark felt his 80 sq. m. apartment was overpriced, other homes in Belmayne peaked at €600,000 for four-bedroom 188 sq. m. houses and €425,000 for 145 sq. m. three-bed units.

Not everybody was enamoured of the display of fashion and flesh on the Malahide Road. The McCann Erickson billboards were subject to an Advertising Standards Authority complaint, which was upheld, with the developer instructed to remove the offending hoarding.

But for Mark, he 'finally had his own place', the starter home that he had worked so hard for, saved so long for and now finally had the keys for.

'I just felt so content'

On the other side of the city, tucked in off the N11 at the junction of White's Cross, is a low-rise high-density gated apartment complex. Long before any of the residential developments that made up this stretch of the Stillorgan Road were built, Byrne's Galloping Green pub held pride of place. It's still there and its name was borrowed by Tudor Homes, who built 118 apartments next door – the last twenty of which went on the market in 1999.

The *Irish Times* property section described the apartments as 'reached through spacious, bright foyers with high-speed lifts and sweeping stairwells. The units are finished out to a particularly high standard with good quality fitted kitchens, wall tiling in kitchens and bathrooms and maple Shaker-style wardrobes. Some of the apartments have two en suite bathrooms.'[1] Prices ranged from £200,000 to £400,000.

By the time 26-year-old Ciara Holland came to buy one of the ground-floor apartments from its original owner, the price was €515,000.

Born in Stillorgan, Ciara attended school and college locally. In her mid-20s she was working and enjoying life, living at home with her parents. 'The desire for me to have my own place', she said half-jokingly, 'was more for my parents. I was perfectly happy living with them, but I think they thought at 26 it was time I moved out.'

Ciara wanted to stay close to family and friends, and looked from Cabinteely to Sandyford to Stillorgan. 'It was 2006, house prices were crazy,' she recalls. 'There was a kind of desperation, were prices going to keep going up?'

Her Special Savings Incentive Account had come to maturity and her parents 'very generously' helped her out.

Coming in €100,000 below most of the other properties she saw, she went for a ground-floor, two-bedroom apartment in Galloping Green. They viewed the property twice. Had the surveyor out. Checked the management company's accounts and sinking fund. 'Everything was fine,' she said.

The apartment blocks are arced around beautiful, landscaped gardens. 'That was the most appealing thing,' remembers Ciara, 'and why my parents loved the complex. It felt really safe, it had secure gates, the gardens were beautiful and really well maintained.'

About three months after she moved in, she remembers coming home after a night out. 'There used to be two wooden swings there ... I sat on the swing ... and I thought how incredibly lucky I was to be in this beautiful development, to own an apartment, I just felt so content.'

Of course, the mortgage payments were steep, at €1,800 a month, and the annual management fees were not far off that. 'Looking back at it now, it was an incredible amount of money,' Ciara recalls, 'but back then it was the norm. €515,000 for a two bed was completely acceptable.'

'It was an amazing feeling'

Almost a decade after Stephanie, Mark and Ciara bought their homes, Aine moved into her apartment in Carrick-mines Green, on the expanding south-west fringe of Dublin county. Though construction of the 180 homes commenced in 2006, the developer, Laragan Developments, went bust in 2008. The appointment of McStay Luby as receiver the following year saw works restart.

When the apartments eventually went on sale in 2016, the *Irish Independent* reported that 'hundreds of prospective buyers showed up' for the launch.[2] Under the headline 'Apartments make the most of near-rural views', the newspaper said that 'the design makes the most of its near-rural setting in Dublin 18, with dual aspects and glass balustrade balconies in some of the units', and with 'wooden floors and polished granite kitchen among their best interior features'. Prospective buyers who may have been concerned at the remote location of the complex were reassured to know that 'each unit comes with its own designated car space and there are plenty of parking spaces for visitors too.'

For Aine, however, price and proximity to family and friends were the deciding factors. She had recently split up with her boyfriend, Alan, and moved back in with her parents. She was 'beyond living with other people and had to live on her own' but couldn't afford to rent. Soon she discovered that buying would be just as difficult.

'I was extremely angry,' she said. 'I was livid at the fact that I had worked so hard to get to a point in my life where I had a very good job with a good salary and that still as a single woman I could not live on my own.'

Luckily for Aine, her parents were able to help and, along with her own savings, they managed to put together a large deposit of €100,000. 'It was still incredibly difficult as a single earner', remembers Aine, 'to purchase a property and if I hadn't had that substantial deposit, I don't think I would have got a mortgage.'

Though her first memory of being in the apartment was 'the noise from the road' prompting her to think, 'Oh my God what have I done?', she remembers that after moving in 'it was an amazing feeling'.

Shortly afterwards, Aine and Alan patched things up, and two years later they married. The following year they had their first child.

'You can watch the sun set in the evening'

On the other side of the country, in Shannon, County Clare, the 240-unit Brú an Sionna complex was built and sold before the developer Paddy Burke Builders went into receivership in 2010.

Some years earlier, *The Irish Times* had told prospective buyers that Brú was 'worth the investment'.[3] Among the attractions were a number of recently opened Ryanair routes from Shannon to various European cities, and the Westpark shopping centre, under construction at the time.

Indeed *The Irish Times* went so far as to say in its 'verdict' on the 'investment' that Shannon was an 'up-and-coming town [that] has become a more attractive place to live'.[4] Though it did also advise that better value could be found in the town from non-Section 23 tax relief purchases.

But for retired couple Lorraine and Gary Carew, it wasn't the shopping or the flight frequency that attracted them to Brú na Sionna. In fact, living opposite, in a comfortable cottage, they were among the initial objectors to the development.

'When we heard about the apartments,' said Lorraine, 'we went bananas ... I'd seen apartments in Dublin and what happens if they are not managed properly.' So, along with all their neighbours, the Carews duly wrote to the council setting out their opposition. But their concerns fell on deaf ears and the development went ahead.

Gary was originally from Thurles and Lorraine from Dublin. They met working on the ships years earlier. In fact, when they met, Lorraine, who was working as a steward, was only one of two women employed on the vessel. When their time at sea came to an end, Gary got a job with the Department of Communications, first at the Malin Head radio station and then in Shannon. Lorraine worked in car hire and with an auctioneer until her husband 'dragged her screaming from Dublin down to Clare'.

After retirement, the couple started to find their bungalow and its generous gardens too much work, especially after Lorraine developed a back problem. So, they decided to downsize. And there in front of them was a south-facing apartment with a big balcony.

'We never had the sun in the evenings because we lived on a hill, the wrong side of the hill,' remembers Lorraine. 'So, we were saying God isn't that lovely, a lovely sun, sitting out on your balcony and no garden.'

The apartment had been a Section 23 tax relief property that was repossessed by the banks some years before. It had been vacant for a while. While neither Lorraine nor Gary actually liked the aesthetics of Brú na Sionna, the apartment was big and the south-facing aspect was key.

'The apartment itself was really nice,' said Gary.

'I love our apartment, it's like 130 square metres,' interjected Lorraine.

'You've got the sun all day, you are facing south Sunday morning and you watch the sun set in the evening,' concludes Gary.

At €130,000, the price wasn't bad and, with the sale of their bungalow, Lorraine and Gary were nicely set up for their retirement. A spacious sun-soaked apartment requiring little maintenance where they could spend their days together reminiscing about their early romance on the Irish shipping cargo vessel as it criss-crossed the oceans.

CHAPTER TWO

Discovering the Defects

'I was sick, it was pretty sickening.'

Mark moved into his Belmayne apartment just after Christmas 2006. 'I was one of the first residents in this part of the development and the first one in this block,' he said. But as soon as his neighbours started moving in, he realised there were problems with noise transmission between apartments.

'It made it difficult at times,' he recalled. 'People were living around you, particularly if you had someone above you. They weren't doing anything out of the ordinary, maybe playing with their kids. It actually made it difficult to sit in the room and watch TV.'

He recalls a couple living below him with a 'fractious relationship ... the whole building would shake when doors were being slammed.' The noise levels were impacting on his enjoyment of his home and he found himself 'having to leave the flat at times to get away from the noise'.

At first, he thought it was just an issue of the wrong type of flooring. Laminate flooring was not permitted in the development. But even after neighbours laid rugs and carpets, the problems continued.

Initial complaints to the managing agent KPM led to the involvement of the developer, Kitara/Stanley Holdings. Consultants were brought in and tests carried out on some of the vacant and unsold homes. Mark remembers units being stripped out and retrofitted to resolve the problem. On one occasion he was even invited to stand on the ground floor of one of the vacant units while a contractor jumped on the floor above. Asked if the works made any difference, he told the contractor, 'I could see the ceilings flexing … no it didn't sound any better … in fact, I could see the ceiling moving.'

Gradually Mark started to realise that the problem wasn't one of inappropriate floors or acoustics, but that the timber frame building system itself was either 'flawed or not erected properly'.

In 2011 Dublin Fire Brigade carried out a visual inspection of some properties in Belmayne but reported no fire-safety issues. However, the following year a second inspection revealed widespread defects affecting up to 300 homes.

Irish Independent environment correspondent Paul Melia reported, 'hundreds of people will be forced to leave their homes after fire officers discovered a blaze risk at their housing development.'[1] The report said that 'urgent repairs need to be carried out at 270 units' due to inadequate fire stopping. Kitara/Stanley Holdings claimed that the defects had been discovered during 'routine repair work' and that they had contacted Dublin Fire Brigade.

While Kitara/Stanley Holdings undertook to carry out the remedial work as soon as possible, it was NAMA that would cover the initial cost, as the developer's loans had been transferred to the state's 'bad bank' in 2010. NAMA would recoup its funds from rents paid by tenants of the developer.

Though remedial work was carried out on most of the defective units, a number of homeowners didn't trust Kitara/Stanley Holdings to do the work properly and refused access to their apartments. Initially Mark was one of these.

By 2012 Mark was married and his wife was expecting their first child. In light of the serious fire-safety issues, they took the difficult decision to vacate the property and initiate legal action against the developer. 'I was sick, it was pretty sickening,' he said, 'because I spent a lot of money on this place, I put myself into a lot of debt. I just wasn't going to have my pregnant wife living in this place. Should something happen I wouldn't be able to live with myself.' The apartment has remained vacant ever since.

In the years that followed, the development was handed over to the owners, who elected their owners' management company (OMC). Complaints about structural defects persisted, and in 2017 the OMC commissioned Thorntons Chartered Surveyors to 'inspect and prepare a defects report on the development'.[2]

The report noted, 'Greater deterioration and damage ... over what would normally be expected due to poor design, construction and workmanship ... The most serious issues relate to balconies.' It also spoke of 'poor detailing and finishing of the metal/aluminium joinery', incorrect 'joinery fixings' and 'installation of balcony floors', and of insufficient 'rainwater drainage' leading to 'water penetration/dampness'.

The surveyors said, 'A radical overhaul will be required of the various balcony structures inspected, and this will be costly where high level access is required.' The report's summary was littered with phrases like 'poor workmanship', 'inadequate', 'poorly fitted' and 'serious shortcomings', and made clear that in their opinion all of this was 'the responsibility of the original developer/builder'.[3]

Significantly, almost five years after Dublin Fire Brigade discovered fire-safety issues in Belmayne and Kitara/Stanley Holdings promised to remedy the defects, the Thorntons survey also noted 'missing or poorly fitted fire stopping to party walls' and 'absent cavity closing barriers'.

Two years later Jack Horgan-Jones reported in *The Irish Times* that the problems had still not been fixed. One resident said, 'I don't think the problem is any closer to being addressed. I feel it isn't closer to being resolved, and eventually when something does come out or when reports do come out, I feel residents may end up bearing the cost.'[4]

'We were absolutely left in the dark about everything'

Stephanie and Fiachra were keen to start moving into their new home in Priory Hall but quickly realised it wasn't going to be plain sailing. Living in the apartment block next door, they could see the building work slowing down. Roads were unfinished, equipment wasn't going in, and Stephanie distinctly remembers thinking 'there's something going wrong here'.

They got a six-month extension of their tenancy in Grattan Lodge, and eventually, as 2008 came to a close, they got the keys. They were one of the first to move in but very soon realised that the problems were more than cosmetic.

Stephanie recalls a bad storm one night with heavy rain and wind. 'The windows were not only leaking,' she said, 'water was pouring into Oisin's cot.' Soon they found water coming in through the windows downstairs, and the floorboards on the second floor 'were saturated'.

Though Stephanie and Oisin moved back in with her mother for a short while, the young family didn't want to be apart, so they moved back home. Still the communal areas and hallways were completely unfinished. Sockets with uncovered wires were hanging out everywhere. The lift rarely worked, which for a family with a baby living on the fourth floor was more than an inconvenience.

Though she said it was 'very upsetting', Stephanie reconciled herself to the problems. 'We thought everything would be looked after, we thought these were just teething problems.'

But Priory Hall had problems well before the apartments were sold, let alone occupied. In June 2006, *The Irish Times* reported that the building site had been closed following complaints to the High Court by the Health and Safety Authority. The article stated that 'the safety inspector had described the site in Donaghmede as "one of the most unsafe" he had ever inspected'.[5] In one incident a 'woman had to be cut out of her car after a large quantity of mesh fell on it'.[6] The court was also told of 'problems on the site going back to 2004', including 'two near-fatal accidents'.[7]

In a portent of things to come, the barrister acting for the Health and Safety Authority said his client 'would normally seek to agree the voluntary closure of the site but it has no faith that such a closure would bring about the desired change'.[8]

In 2009, on foot of a fire-safety inspection, Dublin City Council evacuated their social housing tenants, as they considered the building 'potentially dangerous'.

Enforcement action was then taken against the developer, Coalport, to address any fire-safety issues in the complex. If they failed to comply, they would be taken, once again, to court.

Despite the action taken by the Dublin City Council housing department, the Dublin City Council Fire Authority said that it was 'not going to tell people [owner-occupiers and private rental tenants] to move out'.[9]

Though there had been a residents committee up and running for some time, Stephanie worked nights managing a restaurant, so didn't attend much. Nevertheless, once the rumours about the fire safety started to emerge, she became more active.

'None of us had ever experienced anything like that,' she said. 'We didn't have a clue what was going on. We were absolutely left in the dark about everything.' Fiachra did his best to patch the place up and make it as safe as possible, but when asked if she felt safe living in Priory Hall, Stephanie said, 'It didn't feel like it was going to fall down, but in the case of fire? Yeah, we were terrified, absolutely terrified. For that period of time there were very few nights that we actually slept for a full night.'

It was about that time that their second child, Cerys, was born, but instead of experiencing the joy of a new daughter, Stephanie described it as a 'really difficult time'. Eventually Stephanie and the children moved back into her mother's. Because the security in the block was poor, Fiachra stayed in the apartment to ensure it wasn't broken into.

Despite three separate fire notices having been served on Coalport in 2009 and a schedule of remedial works agreed with Dublin City Council in December of that year, the developer failed to comply with the enforcement action.

Almost two years later the council asked the High Court to evacuate the building.

Donal Casey, a fire officer, told the court that defects in the external walls could see fire spread through an entire block in minutes. He told the judge that the entire external wall of the development would have to be removed in order to make the building compliant with fire-safety regulations – work that he estimated would take a month to complete.[10]

On Friday, 14 October 2011, the High Court approved the request for evacuation, effectively rendering the 256 residents of Priory Hall, including Stephanie, Fiachra, Oisin and Cerys, homeless.

'There is nowhere for us to go for advice'

While residents in Priory Hall and Belmayne discovered the problems with their homes shortly after moving in, Ciara Holland and her neighbours in Galloping Green had been living there for over a decade before discovery.

During the summer of 2018, rumours started going around the complex that there were some issues which would need remediation. Ciara remembers hearing that 'the sinking fund would cover it or if not, there would be a small levy'.

In December residents were called to an information meeting just before Christmas at which a presentation from Omega Surveying Services was made. Ciara said, 'There were leaks in Block 2 ... no fire stopping in some apartments ... problems with fire doors ... huge gaps.'

The language in the presentation was more technical – it listed problems including 'pipe penetrations not fire rated', 'open external cavity walls' and 'protected entrance hallways not carried up to the ceiling'.[11]

At the core of the issue were significant fire-stopping defects that urgently needed remediation. Ciara 'couldn't believe it … the timing … just before Christmas … the room was shocked'. The meeting was also informed that the works were significant and neither the sinking fund nor a small levy would cover the cost.

Ciara remembers having a lot of questions and wanting to get the costings independently verified. A second meeting was held in January to vote on what course of action to take. One woman proposed protesting at the offices of Tudor Homes, the developer responsible. Ciara recalls that this was met with a strong view that 'we don't want this going public … it's going to affect the value of our property and … if the fire officer finds out we will have to evacuate'.

Having paid so much for the apartment and worked so hard to cover her mortgage and management fees, Ciara was angry. 'There is a massive problem with this whole process,' she said. 'There is nowhere for us to go, for advice or to talk things through. I was frantically Googling. You feel so abandoned. When they're telling you not to go public, not to the fire officer or Dún Laoghaire–Rathdown County Council, nobody, you're left in this limbo. You actually don't know what the right thing is to do. You know you are being wronged but you don't know where to go for advice.'

As she was now the mother of two young children, she was also terribly conflicted. 'It goes against everything you believe in. We are actually living in somewhere that's so dangerous that we don't want to tell the fire officer in case he evacuates us! I want to be evacuated if the building isn't safe enough. I have two little girls, there is a lady living above with mobility issues.'

'We were out of our depth entirely'

In December 2017 Lorraine and Gary received a notice for the annual general meeting (AGM) of the Brú na Sionna management company. They had heard that the meeting was to discuss an increase in the service charge. Lorraine initially thought this could be a positive as it may lead to an improvement in the maintenance of the block.

The meeting was well attended, but the news wasn't about maintenance. Residents were told of significant fire-safety defects that had to be remedied immediately and would cost thousands of euros. Lorraine remembers, 'We were told that everyone has to pay €10,000 or the place will be closed down ... they gave us the scare tactics.'

'I was terrified,' she said. 'If there was a fire where would we go?' With Gary's occupational pension, they wouldn't be entitled to any rental support, nor could they afford market rent.

Gary remembers Lorraine coming back from the meeting 'obviously very upset'.

'There was a lot of information thrown at the group,' he said. 'I had no idea of the implications of what was about to happen ... we were out of our depth entirely. We had no idea what was going on.'

It later transpired that the fire-safety defects had been discovered earlier in the year and the management company had installed fire marshals in July 2017. In November, Clare County Council had been notified of fire-safety issues and a fire-safety inspection was carried out. Speaking to

RTÉ News in February 2018, Clare chief fire officer Adrian Kelly said that while short-term solutions had been put in place, works would need to be carried out 'as quickly as possible'.[12]

When asked if she had any idea of the fire-safety defects when purchasing the apartment, Lorraine said she 'never heard a word'.

'Our solicitor looked over it, everything seemed OK, the management company seemed OK, the sinking fund was in place, everything seemed fine,' she said.

Nonetheless, she subsequently discovered that issues had been discussed at an AGM in 2015, which leads her to strongly suspect that the seller of her apartment had been aware of problems. 'Oh yeah, they knew,' she said, 'without a doubt they knew.'

One of Lorraine's neighbours, Rabin Hendoui, who had been renting in Brú, signed a contract to purchase the apartment on the day after the December 2017 AGM. He told Mick Clifford of the *Examiner*, 'I made the final payment on 8 December and signed the last contract on 19 December … When I brought it up [the fire-safety defects] they said I was living here and that I knew what the problem is, but nobody ever told me.'[13] He described the first few months living as an owner-occupier as 'hell'.[14]

'There's far more people embroiled in this'

When Laragan Developments went bust and work on Carrickmines Green stopped, McStay Luby were appointed as receivers. Subsequently NAMA provided funding to complete the development. So, when Aine purchased from the receiver in 2016, as far as she was concerned they were buying from NAMA. 'That did provide me with some assurance,' she said, 'because they are government affiliated.'

The fact that the purchase price was lower than other developments did give Aine an 'inclination' that the apartment may have some issues. 'In the surveyor's report,' she said, 'there were minor issues ... but there was nothing major that would have indicated that it was as bad as it currently is.'

Almost a year after she had moved in, an AGM was called and residents were informed of significant structural defects in the complex. Alan described the meeting as 'tense'. Aine said, 'People in the meeting were frightened and anxious.' Alan recalls that they were told of 'water ingress issues in the car park, more serious defects in other buildings with regard to lift operation, the lift would be out of action for three or four months'.

The meeting received a briefing from Scott Murphy Chartered Surveyors, who had undertaken inspections of some common areas at the request of the OMC. According to Olivia Kelly of *The Irish Times*, residents were told of 'defects including fire doors with excessive gaps, missing fire stopping materials, an absence of smoke seals, fire escapes that were too narrow, and diving walls – designed to stop the spread of fire – where holes had been packed with insulating material instead of being fixed'.[15]

'And then there was the fire-safety issue,' said Alan, 'which was the biggest part because if there is a fire in our building ... the fire would come up straight away.' Aine described being 'very fearful and ... stupid ... I did everything by the book'. Alan said that he 'was quite angry'. 'I felt that it was just unacceptable. It was stressful. We were planning to start a family ... so we wanted to have a safe environment to bring up a child.'

In fact, Aine and Alan had been planning their family since they got back together earlier in the year. They both had good jobs with decent pay, and as the apartment was quite small, they were already thinking of moving on. Alan described feeling 'trapped and tied down to the development', unable to 'upgrade and move on and give the child somewhere to go out and play on the road'. For Aine it was the realisation that 'we won't be able to sell for a long time which means we are stuck in a defective building' that made her feel 'very powerless'.

But the couple's overriding emotion was anger. 'I'm angry at the developer,' Aine said, 'and at some level at the receiver, [but] it was only when my father said that "you bought that place from NAMA" that I started to think, there's far more people embroiled in this and that makes me really angry.'

CHAPTER THREE

The Developers' Response

'Tudor Homes develop fire-defective homes'

In most cases in life, if you buy something and discover it is defective, you bring it back to the shop and get it replaced or your money back. Badly made products are replaced, recalled or refunded every day of the week. Surprisingly this does not apply to what for most people is the single biggest purchase of their life: the family home.

Since the passing of the Building Control Act in 1990, developers and builders are responsible for ensuring that the homes they build and sell are compliant with building and fire-safety regulations.

So, when Ciara Holland was being told at the Galloping Green AGM that her apartment was not compliant with fire-safety rules, she asked, 'What have you done with the developers and architect?'

She was told, 'Both of them have been contacted. The architect never replied and Tudor Homes responded saying the statute of limitations applied so they weren't responsible.'

Tudor Homes have a reputation for being a high-quality developer of upmarket residential homes. In 2006 the *Irish*

Independent property section gave the company a glowing review, including their Galloping Green complex, claiming:

> The reputation of Tudor Homes has gone from strength to strength. With the ground-breaking Sion Hill development in Blackrock, Galloping Green in Stillorgan, White Oak in Clonskeagh and latterly Brennanstown in Cabinteely the company has brought the latest construction technologies to their projects, offering stylish developments to the house-buying public. They pride themselves on their holistic approach to building – they gather around them a first-class team of town planners, architects, landscapers and craftspeople.[1]

According to the Company Registration Office, they were first registered in 1981 and list brothers Martin and Walter Browne as the directors. Their registered office is in Lonsdale House, Avoca Avenue, Blackrock. Both brothers are listed as directors of fourteen other companies, mainly dealing in property, with six registered in the Isle of Man, one in Jersey and the remainder in Ireland.[2] Interestingly Martin Browne is listed as a director of the National Housebuilding Guarantee Company Ltd, the body that owns HomeBond.[3] The Citizens Information website described HomeBond as follows:

> The National House Building Guarantee Scheme is a scheme established by the Construction Industry Federation and the Irish Home Builders Association, in conjunction with the Department of the Housing, Planning, Community and Local Government. It

ensures that proper building standards are maintained and protects purchasers by underwriting any major structural defects in new homes.[4]

As a general rule, HomeBond insurance is meant to protect owners from structural defects in their homes for up to ten years. However, the nature of the cover and the conditions on the warranty have been widely criticised. In many cases of Celtic Tiger latent defects, having HomeBond provided no remedy for owners.

The most recent accounts filed by Tudor Homes are for the financial year up to 31 March 2018. They show that the company and its directors are in a very healthy position. Total assets less liabilities were €26,546,764, with the same sum listed as equity attributable to the directors.[5]

The company is also one of the key landowners in the Cherrywood Strategic Development Zone (SDZ) in Dún Laoghaire, with a proposed €130 million development of 367 residential units. The overall SDZ is set to deliver more than 8,700 new homes in the coming years. In order to facilitate the delivery of these much-needed houses and apartments, the Department of Housing, Local Government and Heritage and Dún Laoghaire–Rathdown County Council are investing €15.19 million from the Local Infrastructure Housing Activation Fund (LIHAF) for what is known as 'common infrastructure', including a road and bridge at Druids Glen and a new N11 junction.[6]

Page 62 of the government's 2016 housing plan *Rebuilding Ireland* describes LIHAF as a fund to 'relieve critical infrastructure blockages' that will assist in the 'provision of housing at a lower price point'. The central point of this €200 million-plus fund is to secure an 'accelerated pace of delivery' with 'affordability built in'.

Nevertheless, from the detail of the LIHAF funding proposal for Cherrywood, it is not clear whether there were any 'infrastructure blockages'. Nor does it appear that the developers would not have been able to fund the road, bridge and junction themselves. It is also unclear what affordability dividend has been secured in return for this taxpayer-funded infrastructure.

The Department of Housing documentation says there is an 'agreement to facilitate circa approx. 5% extra affordable housing on site'.[7] While no price is mentioned, it is expected to be in the €320,000 range for an average two-bed apartment.

For Ciara Holland, the refusal of Tudor Homes, a very profitable company benefiting from considerable state infrastructure grants, to take responsibility for the defects in Galloping Green 'was just so enraging and so unjust'. She just 'couldn't let it sit'. It is also widely believed that some of the properties in Galloping Green are owned by the directors of Tudor Homes or members of their family, making matters worse. 'The directors are said to own a number of apartments ... you could see that from the proxy voting when the vote came for the fire defects in January.'

While searching online, Ciara came across a legal challenge to a planning permission granted by Dún Laoghaire–Rathdown County Council to Tudor Homes for its portion of the Cherrywood SDZ development. 'So, I thought,' remembers Ciara, 'OK, brilliant I would protest outside the court.' She contacted Tudor Homes by email, saying that 'they have built defective homes' and asking them to engage with residents 'to try and remedy the situation'.

Ciara also made clear that 'if they didn't, I would be going public and would go to their next court hearing. No reply! So, I sent them pictures of the posters we would be holding. No reply!'

On 26 November 2019, Ciara and a few others stood outside the court with posters that read 'Tudor Homes Develop Fire Defective Homes'. As a mother of two children holding down a full-time job, Ciara had never protested before. 'I don't have the time for this,' she said, but 'I do it because I feel so passionately about it'. Tudor Homes still haven't responded to her emails.

'Why should we have to bail him out?'

Paddy Burke Builders Ltd once employed over one hundred people. The Lisdoonvarna-based construction company was founded in 1987 and described itself on its LinkedIn page as having

> continually expanded to become one of the largest contracting firms based in the Mid-West. It has established, and maintains, a reputation for providing a quality product to the client, on time, and at the best possible value. We have a vast range of construction experience having completed countless residential, industrial, educational, medical, recreational, and civil engineering projects.

With a trading address listed on the Companies Registration Office website as Pamdohlen House, Doovadoyle Road, Limerick, the developer had been involved in projects including the Clare County Museum, the Burren Art

College, the Doolan Hotel and Kilteel Bay Hotel, as well as commercial and residential projects in Counties Clare, Galway, Tipperary and Limerick.[8]

The first sign of trouble for Paddy Burke came in 2010 when, according to a report on Clare FM, Clare County Council terminated its contract with the builder for an affordable housing scheme, Glaise na Rinne in Shannon. The local authority claimed that the builder had failed to comply with the terms of the contract.[9]

A sub-contractor, Conrock Ltd, who had been brought onto the job by Paddy Burke Builders in late 2009, claimed that he was owed €42,000 for works carried out.

Two months later, the Clare-based journalist Gordon Deegan, writing in *The Irish Times*, reported that the company had been placed in receivership.[10] A dispute arose over accounts filed by Paddy Burke in 2008 in which he valued ongoing projects at €18.8 million. However, chartered accountants Michael Nagle and Co. of Ennistymon said that 'we were unable to obtain sufficient and appropriate audit evidence regarding the work in progress', and that 'we were unable to determine whether proper accounting records had been maintained'.[11]

In 2010 the developer's debts had been transferred to NAMA, who in turn appointed Horwath Bastow Charleton as receivers. Gordon Deegan reported in the *Irish Examiner* that €5 million of debts owed by Paddy Burke Builders to unsecured creditors would not be paid and the value of a number of unfinished sites 'appears in excess of the current market value'.[12]

According to the Companies Registration Office printout there were fifteen separate charges placed against property and assets held by Paddy Burke for debts to Anglo Irish Bank and Allied Irish Bank.[13]

At the time Paddy Burke Builders went into receivership, Brú na Sionna was an unfinished development. The receiver, acting for NAMA, was now responsible for overseeing the completion of the complex and selling the remaining units in order to recoup the debt.

The fact that Paddy Burke got to walk away from the defective properties he built angered Lorraine and Gary Carew. 'We did everything right,' said Lorraine. 'We got an engineer's report, we got the fire cert, everything was fine. So I don't see why Mr Burke is still travelling around the place saying, "Oh I'm bankrupt!" Well so could we be. Why should we have to bail him out?'

At the time of writing, the receiver had control of forty-four unsold apartments. While an institutional investor in Dublin had expressed an interest, the transaction has been paused pending the outcome of a separate legal case involving Glenkerrin Homes and Grant Thornton, the receiver appointed by NAMA and the management company of Maynooth Business Park.

At the centre of that case was a dispute over who should pay the €3 million required to fix a defective car park and, specifically, whether the proceeds from the sale of the final block of the development should be used for this rather than to pay down Glenkerrin's debts to NAMA.

The relevance of this case to Brú na Sionna is whether a similar argument could apply to the proceeds of the final forty-four apartments, namely that rather than being paid to NAMA to offset Paddy Burke's debts to the state's bad bank, the funds should instead be used to cover the cost of rectifying Paddy Burke's defective buildings – and in turn, preventing the cost being borne by the homeowners.

To date Paddy Burke has yet to make any public comment or to explain how it is that his company built and sold properties with such serious defects.

'Where have they gone? Have they disappeared?'

At the height of the boom, Laragan Developments Ltd was at the cutting edge of high-quality, high-price family homes. Newspaper articles advertising their developments ran headlines like, 'High tech homes in Kilmacanogue' and 'Futuristic homes launched in Santry'. There is little doubt that the specs of these developments were impressive, as was the price.

In September 2008, *The Sunday Business Post* ran an article on Laragan's Rock Valley Crescent, County Wicklow. The 295 sq. m. five-bedroom homes were selling for €1.19 million, while larger 317 sq. m. six-bedroom homes were going for €1.4 million. The luxury homes came with German Alno kitchens, Neffor Kupperbush appliances, custom-made wardrobes, thermostat-controlled gas-fired central heating and underfloor heating in the kitchen and utility areas. As if that wasn't enough, they also had centrally managed high-tech entertainment and broadband communications systems, and remote activation of heating and lights by mobile phone.[14]

Two years earlier, on the other side of the city, in Millners Square, Laragan's 'futuristic homes' came with 'telephone, broadband, TV and sound systems which are co-ordinated from a central hub ... access to Sky Plus without a satellite dish [and] pre-wired for a four-room audio integrated system'.[15] The apartments ranged in size from 71 sq. m. to 88 sq. m., while the duplexes were 95 sq. m., all with prices ranging from €375,000 to €415,000.

For company directors Alan and Joseph Hanly, with trading addresses in Elphin, County Roscommon, Laragan Developments was just one small part of a significant business network. The Companies Registration Office lists seventeen separate companies operated by the brothers, ranging from asphalt to engineering and construction, farming, plant hire, livestock and marina management, sales and quarrying. The brothers also owned and ran two beautifully restored hotels, Lough Rynn Castle in County Leitrim and Kilronan Castle in County Roscommon.

According to Ian Keogh of *The Sunday Business Post*, 'The Hanly Group comprises six autonomous firms specialising in six different areas of quarrying and construction. According to the most recent accounts for Laragan Holdings, the main company in the Hanly Group, it had revenues of €127 million in 2007, but recorded a loss of €432,000.'[16]

Laragan got into difficulty when Velfac Ireland sought to liquidate Laragan Developments Ltd in a dispute over payment for a glazing contract. The company owed creditors in the region of €11 million. Anglo Irish Bank, Allied Irish Bank and Bank of Scotland had outstanding loans of €60 million and in mid-2009 sought to put together a rescue package. The proposal, drafted by examiners in Grant Thornton, would have seen 70 per cent of the company's outstanding tax liabilities written off, creditors paid between 14 per cent and 20 per cent of their debts, and Alan Hanly reclassifying a €62 million advance to the company as a subordinated loan.[17]

In March 2009, the High Court ruled that the company had 'deliberately misled the court by claiming solvency'.[18] In July the court rejected the examinership proposal and the company was placed into liquidation.

While substantial charges were placed against the assets of the Hanly brothers' companies, portions of their businesses continued to trade. For Aine and Alan in Carrickmines Green, the developer's losses are of little concern to them. 'Our developer has gone bust,' said Aine, 'but does he still have properties in this development? Does he have properties elsewhere in the world? Is he living a fabulous life? If so, he should be made to pay for the defects.' She is angered by the fact that the people she believes are responsible for the defects in Carrickmines Green can 'go off and live their life, probably in luxury'.

Alan shares Aine's anger but wants to know, 'Where have they gone? Have they disappeared? Have they set up a new company … the seller is gone now; he's potentially set up a new company somewhere else.'

When Laragan Developments went into liquidation, up to 157 creditors were out of pocket. A further ninety-five apartment purchasers lost their deposits of between €15,000 and €20,000 when sales in Millners Square and Carrickmines Green fell through.

In January 2010, journalist Ronald Quinlan caught up with Alan Hanly at his 53-acre estate in Strokestown. In an article titled 'Builder is Laughing with Mock Mansion', after detailing the widespread financial losses resulting from the collapse of Laragan Developments, the *Irish Independent* writer concluded, 'But for Mr Hanly himself there is a safe haven from life's troubles in remote Roscommon – where home sweet home is this mock-Georgian mansion.'[19]

'It does gall me that they have been able to walk away'

The *Irish Times* property section headline beamed 'Family friendly Belmayne has designer touch'.[20] The new suburb off the 'much improved Malahide Road' promised twelve different house styles, 'a library, two schools, a town centre, its own child-friendly park as well as the usual mix of shops, bars, a creche and a medical centre'.[21]

In 2007 a 97 sq. m. three-bed home would set you back €425,000, with a larger three-storey family home costing as much as €470,000. At the top end of the development, considerably larger four-bed homes up to 188 sq. m. ranged from €515,000 to €600,000.

Belmayne was the epitome of the Celtic Tiger. The developer, Stanley Holdings, had its origins in Shannon Homes, established by Joseph Stanley during the 1970s. Joseph senior's sons all went into the development business, with Michael Stanley establishing Stanley Holdings in 2005.

The building contract went to L.M. Developments Ltd, headed up by Leo Meenagh and Donal Caulfield. Described as 'bling incarnate' by Kathy Sheridan and Frank McDonald in *The Builders*, Caulfield and his Belmayne project oozed the hubris of the Celtic Tiger at its apex.[22] Beneath the €2 million information centre with €60,000-worth of olive trees to induce would-be first-time buyers lay a mountain of debt financing both the new development and Caulfield's penchant for luxury cars, five-star hotels and foreign holidays.

Interviewed in 2007 for *The Builders*, Caulfield admitted he was 'sitting on several hundred million euro in loans and didn't see the slump coming'.[23] Within two years Ulster Bank would call in €7 million in debt and appoint a receiver to L.M. Developments. Laura Noonan reported in the *Irish Independent* that L.M. Developments' parent company, Vue Three Sixty, had loans of €290 million to 'unspecified banks in 2009'.[24]

In 2011 Colm Keena reported in *The Irish Times* that Caulfield and Meenagh's company Belmayne Ireland Ltd had reported losses of €129.8 million in 2009 and 'wrote down the value of its residential stock and development land by €130.5 million during the year to €52.2 million'.[25]

For the residents of Belmayne, however, it wasn't the fortunes of the developers that were causing them concern. At the end of 2011, listeners to RTÉ's *Liveline* programme heard claims that the apartments had building defects. Stanley Holdings responded swiftly, rejecting the accusations and saying, 'an individual purporting to be a fire safety expert made a number of statements alleging that the Belmayne development is not in compliance with building and fire safety regulations. We would like to state beyond any doubt whatsoever that these claims are completely false.'[26]

Stanley Holdings' defence of their development was backed by Dublin Fire Brigade, who claimed that a senior fire engineer who inspected the complex was 'at no time shown any deficient construction'.[27]

Nevertheless, only a few months later, a second inspection by Dublin Fire Brigade discovered significant deficiencies in the fire stopping. There were gaps between the walls where firebreaks should have been placed to stop the spread of smoke and fire. The chief fire officer sought to reassure the owners and tenants of the 270 units that 'the defect identified does not warrant any resident having to move out of their homes'.[28]

Following consultation with Dublin City Council and the Dublin Fire Brigade, Stanley Holdings agreed a programme of remediation. But some residents were unhappy that work was to be based on fire reports commissioned by the developer. Their demand for a full independent inspection fell on deaf ears.

While work commenced, some owners, including Mark, refused to allow the contractor appointed by Stanley Holdings onto their property and opted instead for what has become a ten-year legal challenge.

As with L.M. Developments Ltd, the debt of Stanley Holdings' parent company, Kitara Ltd, was by now transferred to NAMA. In order to ensure the sale of the remaining vacant properties, NAMA loaned funds to Stanley Holdings to complete the remediation works, which the developer then paid back from rent charged on these properties. The issue of who would cover the cost for the private homeowners was unclear.

Social housing landlords were also impacted by the defects. In 2009, three approved housing bodies – Clúid, Hail and Sonas – acquired units in Belmayne. Along with additional tenancies managed on behalf of Dublin City Council, they were initially responsible for 134 properties.

By 2010 this had increased to 236 tenancies. In 2019 *The Irish Times* reported that Clúid had 'already spent €300,000 on repairs addressing past construction failings' and had an additional bill of €150,000 for roof repairs.[29]

Despite the initial remediation by Stanley Holdings, concerns over structural defects continued, particularly with respect to the homes built with timber frames. At least six separate reports from 2011 to 2019 identified problems with fire stopping, water ingress and structurally unsound balconies. In a comprehensive summary of the case, *Irish Examiner* journalist Mick Clifford summarised five of these reports as follows:

Thornton Chartered Surveyors 2017

'Serious shortcomings were noted in respect of missing or poorly fitted fire stopping to party walls. In some instances, we noted absent cavity closing barriers where we managed to view or gain close access to partly inspect cavity wall spaces.

'A concern in relation to the above is that if these elements of fire stopping and fire construction which are easily visible without carrying out an intrusive survey have been carried out to such a poor standard, there is every likelihood that such fire safety elements which are concealed by construction are to an equally inadequate standard.

'An intrusive investigation would be required to ascertain the full extent of the problem in this regard.'

McCartney Smyth Fire and Safety Consulting 2017

A service riser inspected 'does not appear to be adequately constructed to achieve the required fire resistance for the walls and it looks like flammable expand-able foam was also used'.

On fire doors, it found one instance where 'a gap between the fire door and the masonry construction has been filled with flammable expandable foam instead of fire-stopping material'.

Robin Knox and Associates 2014

(Conducted on one dwelling within the complex)

'The lack of proper fire resisting construction and assembly is a MAJOR DEFECT and it appears to me that ANY similar dwelling or building part in this development is a potentially dangerous building. There is an imminent and grave danger to anyone in or around them for any purpose whatsoever.'

McCormack Brunkard Associates 2012

'On inspecting the property, I identified a number of potential fire spread risks. Pipes penetrating compartment floors are not fire stopped. Plaster board construction to compartment floors and ceilings are not staggered, tapped and jointed as per the manufacturer's specification.

'Double layered wall slabs and ceiling slabs providing one-hour protection do not meet and they are not taped, staggered or jointed as per the manufacturer's specification. I recommend an independent fire safety test should be carried out on the construction of the compartment floor build up in an accredited laboratory.'

Noel C Manning and Associates 2011

'FIRE SPREAD RISKS — Wall cavities are not closed. Penetrations through compartment floors not fire stopped. Party / separating walls (spandrel panels) incomplete in their assembly and are not fire stopped.'[30]

A further report on balconies was commissioned by the management company O'Connor Property Management in 2019.[31]

In 2014 Mark eventually allowed contractors acting on behalf of Stanley Holdings to access his property and address the fire-stopping issues. However, further problems were discovered. Mark became increasingly critical of the developer's response to the structural defects, believing that they had been aware of far more problems from the outset. While most people tried to get on with their lives, a small group had refused to accept that the developer had done enough and opted for legal action.

In a decision that he readily admits is 'not for the faint-hearted', Mark insists that those responsible for building defective homes must be brought to book. Sitting in his dusty and cold vacant apartment in 2019, he told me that 'there are regulations there that are in statute, that need to be adhered to'. He insists that failure to comply with self-certification rules shouldn't mean developers get off the hook.[32] 'The fact that you don't inspect doesn't mean that you can ignore the regulations,' he insists. 'The regulations are there; you are supposed to build according to regulations, if you don't you are breaking the law,' he concluded.

Part of the problem, of course, is establishing who is actually breaking the law. Belmayne, like many other developments, involves a cluster of companies, contractors, subcontractors and individuals. While Stanley Holdings and L.M. Developments Ltd are publicly recognised as the developers, they are trading names for other entities including Kitara Developments Ltd (with Caulfield and Meenagh listed as directors), Kitara Ltd (with two Stanley brothers listed as directors), Belmayne Ireland Ltd (again with Caulfield and Meenagh listed as directors) and Belmayne Management Company Ltd (again with two Stanley brothers listed as directors).

A decade on from discovering the defects in his Belmayne home, Mark continues his legal action. L.M. Developments Ltd director Donal Caulfield has spent much of this time working through his debts with NAMA. Meanwhile Stanley Holdings founder Michael Stanley was first out of the traps in the post-crash environment, establishing Cairn Homes in 2015 with his brother Kevin Stanley and business partner Alan McIntosh.

Their 2019 annual report lists 'optimal customer experience' as among their strategic objectives and 'designing and building high quality homes ... that people will love living in'.[33] The report notes a revenue of €435.3 million, with a gross profit of €85.3 million and an operating profit of €68 million for that year, the last of which was up 28 per cent in 2018. Cairn Homes developments have also benefited from millions in taxpayer-funded infrastructure funding under the LIHAF programme.[34]

Despite the impact of Covid-19 both on construction and sales, Cairn performed well in 2020. Their preliminary report for that year on their website indicates a net sales value of €307 million, a revenue of €262 million and an operating profit of €24 million. While this is down significantly on 2019, the company was bullish about its expectations for 2021.

Ironically for residents with significant latent defects in Belmayne, Cairn Homes are currently on site with a major development immediately beside Belmayne. When asked how this makes him feel, Mark says:

> I'm not anti-business. I'm a businessman myself. They are entitled to set up businesses and employ people, you need that for an economy. It does gall

me that they've been able to walk away from poorly built developments without any accountability at all. I wouldn't say that they're not entitled going to earn a living and get paid. But I think government needs to take a close look at people that they hand contracts out to. I think these people need to be held accountable. They're hiding behind legal mechanisms that enable them to walk away from this sort of stuff. If there was more accountability at construction time, I think you'd remove an awful lot of the problems to begin with.

'Any corner that could have been cut was cut'

'What would I apologise for?' a defiant Tom McFeely asked the BBC NI Spotlight reporter Ciaran Tracey in an exclusive interview in February 2014.[35] He denied that Priory Hall was a 'shoddy building', saying that 'I don't think it's any different than most of the other buildings in Dublin.'

He insisted that it shouldn't have been evacuated 'because it's not the firetrap they said it was'.[36] When asked to comment on the tragic death of Priory Hall homeowner Fiachra Daly the previous year, he said, 'I am not to blame for his suicide', insensitively adding, 'Why didn't everybody else not commit suicide in Priory Hall, what was the difference there?'[37]

McFeely was a self-made man. The Dungiven, County Derry native and former republican political prisoner and Long Kesh hunger striker had started working on building sites after leaving jail. He went on to build an impressive property empire including apartment developments in west and north County Dublin and County Louth, and interests in the Plaza Hotel and Square Shopping Centre in Tallaght. He also owned houses and land in a number of other locations. He was reported to have paid €4.5 million for his five-bedroom family home, Coolbawn, on Dublin's prestigious Ailesbury Road.

Though Priory Hall wasn't the only defective development built by his company Coalport, it was the most high-profile and ultimately proved his undoing.

From the very start, the Donaghmede apartment block was mired in controversy. *The Irish Times* reported significant safety breaches during construction in 2006 following 'two near-fatal accidents'.[38] Nonetheless, this paled into insignificance as residents and property owners discovered the depth of the structural defects.

On foot of an inspection by a Dublin fire officer in 2008, a protracted legal battle ensued as the city council attempted to force McFeely and his business partner Larry O'Mahony to rectify the building's many problems.

The seriousness of the fire-safety issue led Dublin City Council to evacuate their own social housing tenants in 2009. However, as the fire-safety notice issued in September 2009 gave Coalport a number of months to rectify the works, private homeowners were not required to evacuate. In fact, many were not even aware that the city council had evacuated their tenants.

In August 2010, Irish Nationwide appointed a receiver to Priory Hall, suggesting that Coalport was no longer in a position to finance the remedial works.[39] As matters deteriorated, the High Court issued an evacuation order in October of that year. Coalport's assets were frozen and the company was given until 28 November to complete the first phase of the works, with all remediation to be finished by the end of January 2012.[40]

Nevertheless, clearly unable to finance the €7.3 million-worth of repair works, Coalport was ordered off the site by the High Court and Dublin City Council appointed a new contractor to undertake the works.[41] McFeely was sanctioned with a €1 million fine and three-month jail sentence for failing to comply with the earlier rulings.[42] Luckily for the developer, this decision was subsequently overturned.

As McFeely fought with lenders, NAMA and the courts, Priory Hall homeowners were living in temporary accommodation while paying mortgages on defective properties that were not safe to occupy. The developer's attempt to file for bankruptcy in the UK failed, but he was eventually declared insolvent in Ireland in 2012.

Only months after the residents of Priory Hall finally secured a deal that would allow them to walk away from their former homes debt free, NAMA moved on McFeely's assets and seized his trophy home in Ailesbury Road, leading to the discovery of €200,000 in cash hidden behind the bath.[43] The *Irish Independent* reported that McFeely's companies owed up to €200 million to NAMA and a further €500,000 to the Revenue Commissioners.[44]

In June 2016, the High Court extended McFeely's bankruptcy to May 2020 'over "very grave" failures to co-operate with the bankruptcy trustee'.[45] However, only months earlier, he was reported to be planning a return to development in the UK, having exited bankruptcy there in June 2015.[46] Having exited bankruptcy in Ireland in 2020, he is now free to resume development.

The rogue developer was in the news in December 2020 for alleged breaches of planning rules. McFeely was carrying out demolition works on a six-bedroom property in Belfast, which he claimed not to own.[47] Residents complained to Belfast City Council's planning department that the removal of trees and a 'historic fence' was not in line with planning rules. The council wrote to McFeely urging him to cease the works.

Priory Hall has now been rebuilt and rebranded, and it is home to a new set of residents. The former owners and tenants have moved on. Except for Stephanie Meehan, whose unimaginable loss can never be undone.

Looking back on the entire episode, she still can't understand how any developer responsible for buildings with defects can be allowed back on a site. She told me that she 'spoke to builders on the site, and they said any corner that could have been was cut. They were told to just ignore things, patch things over, you know, they were told to do that.' While she believes that there are many people at fault, ultimately she holds the builder responsible: 'The blame lies wholly at his feet.'

Stephanie is also concerned that developers responsible for buildings with significant fire-safety and structural defects 'are still trading, maybe under a different name'. And she is adamant that 'no builder should be given a certificate to build again without remedying the properties that they have already built, even if they are 15 years old'.

CHAPTER FOUR

Management Companies Struggle

For Stephanie Meehan, buying an apartment in Priory Hall was a temporary measure. 'It wasn't going to be a forever home,' she told me, 'but it would be the first step to having our own house at some stage.'

Across the road in Belmayne, Mark's experience was something similar. He saw his apartment as a 'starter home' bought at the same time he was beginning a relationship with the woman who would become his long-term partner and mother to their children.

With the exception of Lorraine and Gary Carew in Brú na Sionna, whose apartment was bought as a place to retire in the sun, each of the interviewees for this book saw their apartments as a first step, a foot on the ladder, the beginning of a journey to what would eventually lead to their 'forever home'.

The idea of apartment living as temporary is commonplace in Ireland. The most recent census shows that just 7 per cent of households live in some 200,000 apartments across the state. In Dublin almost a quarter of the city's residential stock is apartments. The transitory nature of apartment living is confirmed by the fact that just 20 per cent are occupied by their owners, with the remaining 80 per cent split between private renters (60 per cent) and social renters (20 per cent).

Small clusters of flats were built by local authorities during the 1930s and 1950s, though these always represented a minority of the overall social housing stock. The state's only foray into high-rise, the Ballymun towers, continues to provoke debate long after their demolition.

While some private multi-unit developments (MUDs) were built in the 1970s and 1980s, the real growth started during the 1990s, fuelled by generous tax breaks for buy-to-let landlords and investors.

The first legislation regulating the ownership and management of multi-unit developments wasn't fully enacted until 2014.

When you buy a house, it's very simple. You own the building and everything within the curtilage of your boundary wall. Sometimes there are issues with the ownership of the land where the developer withheld freehold rights, but buying this is a relatively simple if not always affordable process.

The legal ownership of apartment developments is much more complex. During the 1970s a structure known as owners' management companies (OMCs) emerged whereby apartment purchasers became collective owners of the entire development who then in turn leased their individual apartments for periods of up to 999 years. Apartment owners elected directors onto a board and agreed annual service charges and budgets at an annual general meeting. Directors then employed property management agents to run the development.

Nevertheless, during the Celtic Tiger era little of this was understood by the growing number of people who bought and moved into multi-unit developments. They didn't understand that they were not only purchasing their home but taking on a legal responsibility to fund and manage the communal areas, including lifts, corridors, hallways, roofs and, in some cases, public areas within gated communities.

The matter was further complicated by the practice of some Celtic Tiger developers retaining control over both the management company and property management agent long after the majority of apartments had been sold and occupied.

A report on owners' management companies, published by the approved housing body Clúid and the Housing Agency in 2019, highlighted a growing concern both from local authorities and residents from the mid-2000s 'focused on new developments, where control had not passed to the unit owners, where there were building defects, and where many first-time owners of apartments were realising the costs and prohibitions associated with apartment ownership'.[1]

The Clúid/Housing Agency report references a 2008 Law Reform Commission analysis which 'noted that difficulties arose from "a combination of two factors: poor governance arrangements in which some developers retained inappropriate control over MUDs and an understanding deficit among apartment purchasers who seemed unaware of the consequences of buying in a development by contrast to buying a single house"'.[2]

While the theory of OMCs involves 'empowering the home owners and their directors' to manage the development in the interests of all, the Clúid/Housing Agency report acknowledged that this 'is also one of its significant flaws'.[3]

Directors are voluntary, rarely have the experience or skills relevant to the responsibilities of managing 'complicated multi-million euro properties' and as a result 'become over-dependent on management agents or a small number of directors for guidance and influence in decision making'.[4]

In May 2009 the Minister for Justice, Equality and Law Reform Dermot Ahern published the Multi-Unit Developments Bill, promising a 'new deal for apartment owners'.[5] The legislation was designed to 'introduce a comprehensive legislative framework to cater for the specific needs of apartment owners in multi-unit developments'.[6]

The result would be to 'improve the management and maintenance of the internal and external common areas in apartment complexes' by ensuring that developers established 'a property management company and transfer the common areas of the development to it before any apartment in the development is sold'.[7]

The bill took two years to pass through the Oireachtas and became law in April 2011. While broadly welcomed for providing a legal framework for the apartment sector, the legislation had a number of significant flaws. The Clúid/Housing Agency report singles out the failure of the legislation to require 'developers to complete developments to a particular standard and to provide comprehensive latent defect insurance'.[8]

The fact that the transfer of large numbers of management companies to apartment owners took place during the post-2008 recession also left them with serious financing issues. Low levels of compliance with management fees and inadequate sinking funds to deal with both day-to-day maintenance issues and structural repairs were commonplace.

The report identified latent defects as the 'elephant in the room' when it came to the adequacy of sinking funds, commenting, 'The legacy of self-certification and poor building practices up until 2014, but substantially until 2008, is a cost that no owner would have expected to have to fund.'[9]

As developers went bust, established new companies or were protected by the statute of limitations, the legal responsibility for funding remediation of latent defects fell on apartment owners. Voluntary directors of OMCs had a legal responsibility to address fire-safety and structural issues in communal areas. Where receivers, often appointed by NAMA, or professional investors were involved, the potential for conflict was ever-present, with the average owner-occupier wholly unprepared and ill-equipped for what was to come.

A Mixed Bag

Ciara Holland's experience of the management company and property management agent in Galloping Green was, from day one, positive. While the fees were steep, at €2,000, she said, 'it was probably one of the best run management companies.' Wyse Property, the management agent, kept the place 'pristine'. Ciara commended their response time: 'You bring up something and it's dealt with straight away.' The gardens were 'well maintained' with the 'gardener coming twice a week'. Before the discovery of the defects, she 'never had any complaints or any issues'.

Back in Belmayne, Mark's experience was less positive. From the outset he 'didn't feel that it was particularly well run'. The first agent, Keenan Property Management, was replaced by O'Connor Property Management, but he 'never felt that it was run properly'. While 'common areas were relatively clear', he said, 'oftentimes the refuse wasn't collected'. Mark also complained about 'anti-social behaviour', though accepted that 'to a certain extent that was slightly out of their control'. He 'never felt that' he 'was getting value from the management fees'.

Like many apartment owners, none of the interviewees became involved in their management company when they moved in. Some, such as Stephanie Meehan in Priory Hall or Aine in Carrickmines Green, were too busy with work and family to attend AGMs or committees. Others, such as Ciara in Galloping Green, were happy with the service provided so never felt the need. And while Lorraine and Gary Carew in Brú na Sionna felt the complex wasn't being kept to the standard it should have been, they were nonetheless content with their spacious, sun-soaked apartment and paid little attention to the affairs of the OMC.

It was only when defects were discovered that they all started to engage with the legal structures that managed their homes. Some, like Mark, brought the problems to the attention of existing residents' associations and property management agents. In other cases, such as Galloping Green, Brú na Sionna and Carrickmines Green, it was at management company-organised information meetings that residents first learnt of the defects.

In all cases, however, residents soon discovered that the defects themselves were not the only problem they had to deal with. Accessing information, being given enough time to understand that information, working out who to trust, and whether those in positions of authority had conflicts of interest were issues in all five developments.

Information Deficit

It was at an information meeting called by the Galloping Green management company in December 2018 that Ciara Holland was informed of significant fire-safety issues in the development. She was shocked to learn that the full cost of remediation would be €1.9 million and that her family's contribution would be €16,250. It was a few weeks before Christmas; she and her partner were saving for a deposit, as the apartment was now too small for their growing family. She felt the 'costs were too high'.

At a second meeting in January, a formal presentation was made by Omega Surveying Services detailing the works that needed to be carried out. Ciara remembers 'a lot of anger and a lot of hostility in the room'. She said people 'had a lot of questions but had been given scant information'.

Her primary concern was the costings, which she wanted to get independently verified. 'We're relying on the building sector to remedy a situation the building sector created,' she said. 'I just wasn't comfortable not having sight of this.' Despite formally requesting further information on the costings for the work, this was never provided. Emails were ignored and phone calls weren't returned, all of which made Ciara very 'sceptical of the whole process'.

Ciara described feeling totally 'abandoned in the process'. She said, 'There's nowhere for us to go for advice or to talk things through.' So, without the necessary information and despite having voted against the initial proposal until she received full information, she was left with no choice but to eventually pay the full amount for her home to be made safe.

That sense of powerlessness was echoed by Gary Carew in Brú na Sionna. His wife Lorraine had attended the management company meeting in December 2017 at which they were first told about the defects and a possible bill of €10,000. He remembers Lorraine coming home 'obviously upset because there was a lot of information thrown at the group'. He said it is hard for people to understand, 'we were in limbo ... we had no idea of the implications of what was about to happen ... we had no idea what was going on in the background.'

Despite some residents asking for a few weeks to consider the information presented at the meeting that night, Lorraine recalls that the request was refused. 'They gave us the scare tactics,' she said. 'They scared the bejesus out of us.'

In Carrickmines Green, Aine and Alan remember there being 'a lot of tension in the room' at the January 2017 AGM when they were informed of the defects in their building. Alan says, 'the management company were on the defensive from the start' and 'people who were asking questions were kind of shut down'. Aine was also critical of the failure of the management company and agent to understand that 'people were frightened and anxious and there was absolutely no consideration of that emotive element.'

Whether it was in Belmayne, Galloping Green, Carrickmines or Brú na Sionna, the failure of management companies and agents to provide information when requested, delays in providing information and failure to give owners adequate time to process information generated mistrust and conflict.

While Alan was clear that he felt 'no animosity to the directors' in Carrickmines Green, as they had 'a difficult job doing voluntary work', he was less forgiving of the managing agent. But in other developments the relations between owners and directors were much more complicated, as conflicts of interest and perceived conflicts of interest came to the surface.

Conflicts of Interest

Having come to the realisation that the problems in his apartment block were more significant than he first realised, Mark got involved in the local residents' committee. At this stage it was an informal body, but it often had representatives from the managing agent attend. While he didn't feel that the agent, KPM, 'were much help', they did engage with the developer, which led to inspections and discussion of possible remediation.

After about a year and a half, Mark stepped down from the residents' group. He felt that it was 'controlled by certain figures' who were 'in some shape or form aligned with the developer'. 'Anytime we brought up certain issues at the residents' committee meeting,' he told me, 'it was immediately deflected ... We were told that we won't be talking about those issues today because they are being handled by the developer.' Frustrated that some people were 'singing from the same hymn sheet as the developer rather than supporting the residents', he decided to seek redress elsewhere.

In Brú na Sionna things were much more complicated. AGM minutes from as far back as 2011 show that the OMC was dealing with an incredibly complex situation.

Significant defects, including leaking roofs, non-functioning smoke ventilation systems, broken emergency lighting, defective fire alarm panels and damaged tarmac, had been outstanding for some years. Despite these issues having been brought to the attention of the developer Paddy Burke, they remained unresolved. The developer also owed the OMC significant unpaid management fees of €23,600.

The involvement of receivers appointed by NAMA further complicated matters, as their legal mandate was not always aligned with the interests of the owners. Rather, their function was to ensure that creditors of Paddy Burke Builders Ltd, and in the first instance NAMA, were repaid, which led to conflicts over payment of outstanding management fees and disputes over whether the proceeds of property sales should be spent on remedying defects rather than paying creditors.

In 2015 a new board of directors was elected to the OMC. John Callinan became chairperson and, according to the minutes of the AGM, informed those present that he had 'previously worked as Solicitor for the developer [and] had acted for the receiver in a conveyance capacity'. While he sought to reassure those in attendance that he would resign as chair if there was 'a conflict of interest existing between his professional position and the voluntary role on the board', many owner-occupiers remained unconvinced.

The involvement of the County Clare Fire Service in 2017 escalated matters significantly and required the OMC to propose a supplementary budget of €1.25 million, which would require an additional levy on all properties. Disputes arose over whether the levy should be spread evenly across the development or charged according to where the works were required. Lorraine and Gary Carew felt that the small number of owner-occupiers were outnumbered by investors, including some with direct connections to the developer, and were thus getting a bad deal.

Lorraine and Gary Carew and Mark felt badly served by structures that they believed should have been protecting their interests. In both cases they strongly believed that clear conflicts of interest among some involved in those structures undermined the operation of the management companies to such an extent that their only chance of redress could be found in the courts. At the time of writing, those legal battles are ongoing.

Court action is also ongoing between the OMC and a NAMA-appointed receiver in Carrickmines Green. A dispute regarding the handing over of communal areas is delaying the sale of apartments by the receiver, the proceeds of which the OMC believe should be used to remediate the occupied apartments.

The result is even less information being provided to owners, leading to ever greater frustration, and tension between them and the OMC. Aine and Alan talk about 'secrecy' and 'paranoia' preventing the directors from keeping owners fully informed.

For Gary Carew the experience has left him emotionally exhausted. His greatest fear is that the OMC could eventually put a charge on his property for unpaid management fees, defect levies and interest. He says that the fear of losing a part of his home keeps him awake at night – that 'these people could actually take some of my house, this house that I've worked all my life for, the only thing of value that I've got to leave to my kids'.

His view of the OMC is scathing: 'They are the rudest, most ignorant people I have ever dealt with. They have no empathy whatsoever. No feelings for anybody they are dealing with, irrespective of their personal circumstances, their financial situation. They don't care.'

The experiences of Ciara in Galloping Green, Mark in Belmayne, Aine and Alan in Carrickmines and Lorraine and Gary in Brú na Sionna with how their OMC and residents' groups dealt with the issue of latent defects were wholly negative. None of them believe they were provided with adequate information. All of them felt that conflicts of interest between investors, receivers, developers and owners were at play. Trust between them as owner-occupiers and their OMCs and residents' groups, which they believed should be representing their interests, had completely broken down. And they all felt they had no one to turn to for independent advice.

Kath Cottier is the director of housing services for Clúid Housing Association and a director on the owners' management company at Beacon South Quarter, a Celtic Tiger era development with significant latent defects. In December 2020 she told the Oireachtas Housing Committee that 'The various stresses experienced by homeowners are also, in turn impacting on their relationships within the different developments.'[10] She reminded the committee that 'the OMC directors, who are only volunteers after all, have to levy sums against their neighbours. They are deeply unhappy about this and it causes much difficulty for relations.'[11] Cottier emphasised, 'all this stress and strain arises through no fault of any of the people involved, yet they are left to mop up after other people's failings.'[12]

There is no doubt that the lack of information, active support and capacity building from government for voluntary directors of OMCs left many struggling with how best to address the complex issue of latent defects. In other instances, however, directors were clearly motivated by interests other than those of the owners they were elected to represent.

The 2011 Multi-Unit Development Act may have provided a 'new deal' for some apartment owners, but for those struggling with latent defects the legislation wholly failed to cater for their specific needs.

CHAPTER FIVE

The State Fails

'They have absolutely let me down'

Ciara Holland eventually agreed to pay the €16,250 levy to ensure her family's home was made safe. But she had no intention of letting the matter rest there. A wrong had been done and someone must be held accountable.

She decided to contact both Dún Laoghaire–Rathdown County Council and the Dublin Fire Brigade, at first withholding the name of the development, to see what advice or information they would provide.

On 2 July 2019 she wrote to the council's planning department, expressing concern that Tudor Homes Ltd had been granted permission for their new development in Cherrywood, County Dublin. Ciara informed the council that a former Tudor Homes development 'is now subject to a significant Fire Remediation issue' as a result of their failure to 'build the development in line with fire regulations or indeed in line with the Fire Certificate'. And she asked, 'how can they be granted permission for a €130 million development when they didn't comply with previous DLRCOCO requirements?'

The email concluded with Ciara asking with whom she should raise this serious issue, as Tudor Homes 'need to be held accountable and responsible'.

Ciara received a short reply from the council's planning department the following day, asking for further details of the development in question so that they could 'examine your query fully'.

Initially her reply, on 3 July, indicated an unwillingness to provide the name of the development without knowing 'what action would be taken if I do provide the development's name? Is there a process to be followed that will result in this issue being addressed?'

On 4 July the planning department replied, saying that 'without evidence I cannot proceed with your query', insisting that the claim made against the builder is 'a very serious matter and needs to be substantiated in order that the appropriate action can be taken. Otherwise the Council is not equipped to deal with the matter.'

After giving the matter considerable thought, Ciara provided Dún Laoghaire–Rathdown County Council with the name of the development in a reply on the same day. She also offered copies of the engineer's reports if required.

In contrast to the quick responses to her initial emails, once she named the development there was 'radio silence'. Ciara said, 'They acknowledged this is a very serious issue and then just ignored me.'

Reminder emails were sent to the planning department in August, September and November 2019, but no response was forthcoming. On 16 December, Ciara once again emailed the planning department; however, this time she cc'd the then Minister for Housing, Eoghan Murphy, and his Minister for State, Damien English.

Ciara's growing frustration at being ignored by the authorities is evident in the email. She wrote, 'Eoghan Murphy has publicly stated that this is a private contractual matter. It is not. This is a blatant disregard by developers of people's safety.'

On 17 December Ciara received a standard reply from the council's planning department stating that if she wished to make an objection to the Cherrywood application, she would have to pay a €20 fee. The following day she replied again asking for a substantive response to her original email.

Finally, the planning department replied on 15 January 2020. The email set out the provisions of Part VIII of the Building Control Act 1990, which states, '(2) An enforcement notice shall not be served, in respect of the building works concerned after the expiration of the period of five years commencing on the date of – (a) the completion of the building works, or (b) the material change in the purposes for which the building is used.'

The council's planning official concluded, 'Given that the properties concerned were built in the late 1990s and early 2000s the Council does not have the authority to investigate the matters outlined in your e-mail owing to the time that has lapsed since the apartments were completed.'

The December email was not the first to be sent to the then Minister for Housing. Five weeks earlier, Ciara had sent a detailed email to Eoghan Murphy and Damien English setting out the background to the defects at the Galloping Green apartments. She concluded with an appeal to both ministers: 'You grow up and are taught right from wrong, to believe that wrongs will be corrected.' Describing what had happened to the apartment owners at Galloping Green as a 'huge injustice', she made an appeal to the two men who ultimately held the power to do something about this:

> We need the government's help to bring those culpable to justice, they should never be able to build again until they remedy what they have done. Why is your Government permitting this ongoing situation? Why are you not addressing it? ... Your government has set the precedent by helping those with Mica and Pyrite. I don't think that it is appropriate or fair that you cherrypick which defective homes you assist. By ignoring us we will not go away. This injustice needs to be remedied.

But ignore her they did. Neither Eoghan Murphy nor Damien English ever replied to Ciara's emails. 'They don't want to hear the real-life stories,' she told me. 'They have absolutely let me down.'

'The Government could be very much embroiled'

The National Asset Management Agency (NAMA) was set up by the Fianna Fáil government in 2009. Its function was to buy the toxic banking liabilities from the Celtic Tiger period at a discount and, through sale or lease, recoup the billions of taxpayer's monies used to 'purchase' these assets from the banks.

The agency describe themselves on their website as 'an unusual corporate entity', the job of which is to 'recoup at a minimum all of the expenditure incurred by it on acquiring loans, on advancing working capital and on its own costs.

In doing so, it will pursue all debts owed by its debtors to the greatest extent feasible.'

Section 1 of the NAMA Act 2009 sets out the legal functions of the agency, including addressing the threat to the economy, stabilising the financial system, protecting taxpayers and contributing 'to the social and economic development of the state'.[1]

Crucially, however, Section 10 of the act sets a very high bar for all NAMA's commercial activities, as it is obliged to 'obtain the best achievable financial return for the State'.[2] These nine short words were to have significant consequences for apartment owners who purchased their homes from receivers acting on behalf of NAMA.

When Aine was searching for her first home, the *Irish Independent* was telling prospective buyers that Carrickmines Green has 'Penthouse views of the Dublin Mountains'.[3] The feature in their property section said, 'The homes were completed six years ago by Laragan Developments before a receiver was appointed by Nama. The properties were then rented out and, after the tenants gradually moved out, Knight Frank oversaw a complete refit of the units and put them back on the market.'

Strictly speaking NAMA was neither the owner nor the seller of the apartments. They held the debt and had appointed receivers to ensure that that debt was recouped. But NAMA was also funding the completion of the Carrickmines development, and it was ultimately a state agency, albeit one constructed as a special purpose vehicle in which the state held a 49 per cent stake.

So, while NAMA was not responsible for the initial defects in Carrickmines, in the eyes of owners like Aine and Alan, they still had a responsibility to assist in resolving the problems. Aine told me that it was only when her father reminded her she had effectively bought the property from NAMA that she started to realise:

> There's far more people embroiled in this than just a developer and a receiver. And of course, that makes me really angry. Here we are waiting for a potential redress scheme and the Government will be really embroiled in all of this.

At the time of writing, a legal case between the receiver, appointed by NAMA, and the OMC is underway. At the centre of the dispute is the transfer of common areas from the OMC to the receiver for the final block of the development. For the owners, this may be the only chance for them to force the receiver and NAMA to contribute financially to the cost of remediation for the properties sold after 2009.

In January 2020 I wrote to NAMA asking them to outline their involvement with the Carrickmines development since 2009: whether they knew about the defects in properties sold by their appointed receivers; whether they believed they had any responsibility to assist in funding the remediation; and how much money they had made from the sale of these properties. I also asked them to comment on the ongoing legal case.

The agency responded, saying, 'there is an on-going litigation between the appointed receivers and the OMC. NAMA is not a party to this litigation and it not in a position to comment on the matter.' They concluded by adding, 'by virtue of sections 99 and 202 of the NAMA Act, NAMA is prohibited from disclosing the confidential information that would be required to respond to certain other questions raised in your correspondence.'

'NAMA sold the debt'

Carrickmines Green is not the only development with latent defects that NAMA was involved in.

When Brú na Sionna builder Paddy Burke Ltd went into receivership, his loans were with Anglo Irish Bank. These were eventually transferred to NAMA, to whom the receiver was ultimately answerable. The estate was unfinished, and a dispute arose between the management company, Tullyvaraga, and the receiver, Eoin Ryan, as to who was legally responsible for financing the completion of the development.

While the Multi-Unit Developments Act states that the developer is responsible for finishing an estate, it is silent on where legal responsibility lies when the developer has gone into liquidation and a receiver has been appointed.

The *Irish Examiner* reported how owners of the defective apartments viewed the stand-off in February 2018:

> The owners, through Tullyvaraga, felt the receiver should take on the responsibility of the developer to finish the estate and acquire certificates of compliance for the common areas.
>
> The receiver was of the view that this was not his baby. He initiated legal proceedings against Tullyvaraga, which counter-sued for the failure to complete the estate.
>
> At this point, hope still persisted, as Nama was ultimately holding the purse strings. Over the years,

Nama has in a number of instances acted beyond its legal obligation to complete estates that required work.

So, despite pending litigation, the prospect of Nama intervening in the name of social responsibility always existed.[4]

The *Examiner* went on to report that the hopes of owners were then dashed when NAMA sold the Paddy Burke loans to Promontoria Ltd, a subsidiary of one of the world's leading vulture funds, Cerberus.

Conor Glennon, solicitor for Tullyvaraga, told the *Examiner*, 'To the management company's surprise, Nama sold the debt.'[5] With the loans now in private hands, the 'prospect of State intervention' was gone.[6]

When asked why it had sold the debt to a vulture fund rather than finance the completion of the development, NAMA said, 'by virtue of section 10 of the NAMA Act, NAMA is required to obtain the best achievable financial return from its acquired assets. Any strategies employed in relation to the assets were therefore guided by these legal and statutory obligations.'

With the possibility of state support through NAMA now closed off, owners looked to local TDs for assistance. In the case of Lorraine and Gary, this route was also to lead to a dead end.

Describing herself as a 'total die hard' Fianna Fáil supporter and a cumann secretary in Shannon for many years, Lorraine called her local TD for advice. 'The first call I made was to Timmy Dooley's office,' she said, 'and I never got a response.' Gary believed, 'It was all becoming a big hot potato; they didn't want to know.'

The Carews were also critical of Joe Carey TD for offering false hope. In a press release from the Fine Gael TD's website in May 2019, he claimed that the 'Home Building Finance Act could help resolve Brú na Sionna defects.' The bill established a government-backed lending facility for builders. The press release was based on a parliamentary question put to the Minister for Finance, Paschal Donohoe, the previous December.

However, in his reply to the question, the minister made it clear that any lending by Home Building Finance Ireland (HBFI) for the remediation of latent defects would be 'high risk' and 'pose significant issues for lenders in relation to access to appropriate security'.[7] Given that the HBFI legislation required all loans to be 'commercially viable', it is hard to see how it could provide residential developments with significant latent defects and high levels of negative equity with any kind of loan.

This was the only time that Deputy Carey raised the issue of addressing latent defects in the Dáil. According to the official record, not once had he or former deputy Dooley, now a senator, raised the specific issue of Brú na Sionna on the floor of either of the houses of the Oireachtas.

While the Carews felt badly let down by their local TDs, they acknowledged that some local councillors tried to have the issue raised. Sinn Féin's Mike McKee was a case in point – he sought, through motions at the Shannon Municipal District meeting, to apply pressure on the government to assist residents in addressing the defects.[8] Unfortunately the efforts of the councillors were in vain.

'Why Priory Hall and not Belmayne?'

Mark's experience of TDs was more mixed than that of Lorraine and Gary. After he and his partner moved out of the Belmayne apartment, they were living in Marino and wrote to local TDs. Fine Gael's Richard Bruton was 'supportive to a point', Gary said, 'but in the end passed the buck to the Fire Service'. Independent TD Tommy Broughan 'has been somewhat helpful ... bringing up issues in the Dáil'.

Mark singles out the then Fingal county councillor, now TD, Cian O'Callaghan as having been 'very helpful ... particularly with Freedom of Information Requests that have been very helpful with the legal case'. The documents sourced by Councillor O'Callaghan led Mark to question what the Dublin Fire Brigade knew and when.

'Did the Fire Service know the full extent of the problems from their first inspection?' asked Mark. 'When did they come to know about the subsequent issues and why were they not more forthcoming in informing the owners?'

Ultimately, however, political engagement didn't resolve the issue and Mark's legal battle continues. But he believes that the Dublin Fire Brigade have questions to answer. Why did their 2011 inspection not discover any fire-safety defects, while their subsequent inspection in 2012 did?

As Mick Clifford reported in the *Examiner* in 2011:

> [A] 'very senior fire engineer' was sent to survey the complex, according to a letter from the chief fire officer at Dublin Fire Brigade to an apartment owner in the complex. 'At no time was he shown any deficient construction,' the chief fire officer wrote. 'He has looked into the system of on-site supervision and

also into the certificate of completion … I am satisfied
he carried out a diligent and competent investigation
and I concur with his report and conclusions'.[9]

A year later, during a second Dublin Fire Brigade inspection,
'defects were uncovered' leading to the developer remediating
225 properties.[10]

Mark doesn't feel that the Dublin Fire Brigade ever fully
explained the discrepancy between the two inspections.
'They stuck to the narrative that there were no issues in
2011,' he said. 'They can't really explain how suddenly
these issues did appear.'

But the big unanswered question for Mark is why the
government intervened in Priory Hall and not Belmayne.
'I found it quite strange', he told me, 'that they decided
to step in at Priory Hall but not Belmayne.' And while he
accepts that part of the reason is that they 'don't want to
put people out on the street', he also wonders if 'one of the
main reasons is that it would cost them an arm and a leg'.

'We just wanted some hope'

In a speech to the Society of Chartered Surveyors of Ireland
in October 2011, the then Minister for the Environment,
Phil Hogan, was asked whether he believed there were more
defective buildings like Priory Hall across the state. He said,
'I have no doubt there is.'[11] He urged local authorities 'to
step up their enforcement activity … and bring people to
justice', while complimenting Dublin City Council for 'doing
their job properly' in taking enforcement action against
Tom McFeely and his company, Coalport. Despite this, no
one has ever been brought to justice for what happened at

the north Dublin estate, and the role of both Dublin City Council and the Minister for the Environment and his department has been subject to very significant criticism from residents and observers alike.

Dublin City Council first became aware of the defects at Priory Hall in 2009. They evacuated their own tenants on fire-safety grounds to carry out remedial work in December of that year. Incredibly, they did not inform the private homeowners.

On foot of the fire-safety notices being issued by the Dublin Fire Brigade in September 2009, a programme of works had been agreed. However, Coalport failed to deliver. It was a full two years later that Justice Nicolas Kearns was compelled to issue an order to evacuate the development, rendering all 256 residents homeless.

Stephanie Meehan said that the evacuation of the Dublin City Council tenants in 2009 'was done very quietly … it was quite shocking how they put a different value on other people's lives compared to our own'. She is also insistent that homeowners 'weren't made aware of it at the time'. Her strongest criticism, however, is not of the city council but the government, and in particular Minister for the Environment Phil Hogan for his refusal to meet with the Priory Hall owners.

During a Dáil debate on 23 November 2011, Sinn Féin TD Dessie Ellis and Independent TD Tommy Broughan urged the government to meet the residents. Deputy Ellis said, 'It is shameful that the residents of Priory Hall have been refused a meeting with the Minister.' Deputy Broughan urged the 'Minister and the Taoiseach to step up to the plate to become directly involved'.[12]

In response, and speaking on behalf of Minister Hogan, Minister of State Ciarán Cannon said that Minister Hogan 'must respect the independence of the designated statutory authority and cannot interfere in individual cases'.[13] He emphasised that 'neither the Minister nor the Department has a statutory function in enforcement activity'.[14]

In August 2013, almost two years later, and with no resolution in sight, Fiachra Daly took his own life. Stephanie Meehan's powerful letter to the then Taoiseach, Enda Kenny, finally shifted the government's position. They could no longer refuse to get involved.

Stephanie Meehan said that the government's two-year refusal to meet the residents was 'very, very hurtful ... we just wanted some answers, we just wanted hope'. While she was not naïve enough to think that a meeting with Minister Hogan would resolve matters overnight, she said, 'It would have made us feel like the people in power actually cared and are listening to us.'

'The thing is', she concluded, 'they didn't. We were completely let down.'

PART 2

CHAPTER SIX

A Short History of Dangerous Buildings

Tenements Collapse – 1913

At 8.30 p.m. on 2 September 1913 two tenement buildings in Dublin's city centre, housing up to fifty people, collapsed. No. 66 Church Street fell first, with five families trapped inside. Those living in 67, alerted by the disintegration of the neighbouring building, were all able to escape before their homes crumbled to the ground.

A newspaper report, published the morning after, described 'horrific scenes ... as bodies – injured, maimed and deceased – were picked from the rubble of two collapsed tenement buildings.'[1]

The Dorset Street and Tara Street fire brigades, fifty Dublin Corporation workers and priests from the nearby Father Mathew Church worked into the early hours of the morning with 'picks, shovels and crowbars' to rescue people from the rubble.[2]

'At one point,' the newspaper recounted, 'a faint, agonised voice could be heard from beneath the masonry and voices of the crowd were immediately hushed', allowing two survivors to be located and rescued.

Unfortunately, not all were so lucky. At least seven people died that night in Church Street. The youngest was 4-year-old Elizabeth Salmon. Her brother, 17-year-old Eugene, had initially escaped but went back into the building to save his sister. He did not make it out alive.

The overcrowded, unsanitary and unsafe living conditions in Ireland's urban tenements were no secret. But the deaths at Church Street were significant, because only a year earlier Dublin Corporation's Improvements Committee published a proposed scheme for the demolition of the area's tenements and their replacement by workman's dwellings.

The committee had undertaken a study of the tenements in October 1911 and found 'the conditions of human existence in all the Courts and passages comprised in the area as most deplorable'.[3] The report, published in January 1912, deemed the area 'unfit for human habitation' and recommended its replacement with five new wider roads and 246 two-storey cottages.

The fact that two years on from the initial investigation no action had been taken – and worse still seven people were now dead – provoked a public outcry. A fundraising drive by *The Irish Times*, *Evening Telegraph* and *The Freeman's Journal* raised over £2,000.[4]

A committee on housing in Dublin was established by the then Chief Secretary for Ireland, Augustine Birrell, the findings of which were published in March 1914. The report found that 45 per cent of the population of Dublin were living in tenements.[5] Among the recommendations to address the problem were the introduction of licences and compulsory caretakers.[6]

Significantly the committee concluded that 'most of the tenement houses have been allowed to go out of repair, and the difficulty is how to get the owners to put them in repair'.[7] To address this problem, two solutions were proposed: making repairs a condition of the licence and having the corporation, or other bodies on their behalf, undertake acquisition and improvement of the buildings.

The most important outcome of the committee's findings was the Housing (Ireland) Act 1919, which provided a new legal framework for the delivery of urban public housing. The widespread labour agitation on housing issues at the time, coinciding with the 1913–14 Lockout in Dublin, no doubt focused the minds of legislators in Westminster, as 'public housing provision had become an insurance against revolution'.[8]

Tenements Collapse – 1963

Fifty years after the deaths in Church Street, tragedy struck again. Tenement buildings in Fenian Street in the south inner city collapsed on 15 June 1963. Two children died, Linda Byrne aged 8 and Marie Varley aged 9.

A contemporary *Irish Times* report commented that 'Parts of Dublin were literally in a state of collapse in the early 1960s when at least four people were killed by falling buildings.'[9] The report went on to say that an emergency meeting of the council was convened, where a promised ministerial inquiry would be arranged.

In the following days, more than 155 families had to be rehoused because they were living in 'dangerous buildings'.[10] While the number of people living in tenements in 1963 was significantly less than 1913, the condition of those dwellings clearly hadn't improved much.

In the intervening five decades, public housing policy in the state had advanced significantly. All governments from

1922 had invested both in the direct delivery of council housing and in the provision of grants and loans for those building or buying their own homes. Nevertheless, the issue of building standards was a regular feature of housing debates.

During the 1930s, as corporation house building took off in earnest, the practice of 'skinning down' emerged. Councils were provided funding on a per unit basis, which created a perverse incentive to produce a greater number of homes at a lower cost. Under pressure to deliver more homes, corners were cut and standards compromised – the consequences of which were felt by future generations of inner city flat complex residents.

This decade also saw the first significant housing boom since the foundation of the state. In addition to increasing the stock of both public and private homes, it brought into play a relationship between Fianna Fáil and the building industry that would have an enduring impact on housing policy in general, and building control regulation in particular.

Nonetheless, it was during the building boom in the 1960s that this relationship was fully consolidated, as 'The huge State subsidy to the construction industry had created a political system of "powerful organisational influences", which had major consequences for other areas of Irish society and life.'[11]

Two days after the collapse of the buildings on Fenian Street, the Minister for Local Government, Fianna Fáil's Neil Blaney, fielded questions from an angry opposition and the government backbenches.[12] Deputies from Fianna Fáil, Fine Gael, Labour, the Socialist Labour Party and the National Progressive Democrats grilled the minister with questions on the number of dangerous residential dwellings in Dublin and the nature of the inspection regime currently in place. They also urged him to make a formal statement on the Fenian Street tragedy.

Minister Blaney informed the Dáil that he had initiated a public inquiry and that Dublin Corporation was responsible for housing-displaced families.

Deputy Noël Browne criticised the 'archaic powers' of Dublin Corporation and urged the minister to take steps to 'bring into the house whatever legislation he feels is required to deal expeditiously with this matter in the future'.[13]

Minister Blaney replied that a bill currently making its way through the House would increase the powers of local authorities in this regard.

Section 86

The bill in question was the Local Government (Planning and Development) Bill, introduced in July 1962. This was the most comprehensive reform of planning in decades. Over almost one hundred sections, it dealt with county development plans, planning retention applications, acquisition of unsafe buildings and compensation for landowners.

It took fourteen full committee sessions over four months to get through the legislation, which was finally passed by the Seanad on 31 July 1963.

On the final day of the committee sessions, Section 86 of the bill was agreed without any discussion. This small detail tucked into the Miscellaneous section of the bill gave the Minister for Local Government a significant new power: to introduce building regulations.

These regulations would, according to the section, 'prescribe standards (expressed in terms of performance, types of material, methods of construction or otherwise) in relation to all or any of the matters specified in the Fifth Schedule to this Act'.

The Fifth Schedule is important and worth quoting in full:

FIFTH SCHEDULE.

Matters for which Building Regulations may prescribe Standards.

Section 86.

1. Preparation of sites.
2. Strength and stability.
3. Fire precautions (including resistance of structure to the outbreak and spread of fire, the protection of occupants and means of escape in the event of fire).
4. Resistance to moisture.
5. Resistance to the transmission of heat.
6. Resistance to the transmission of sound.
7. Durability.
8. Resistance to infestation.
9. Drainage.
10. Ventilation (including the provision of open space therefor).
11. Daylighting (including the provision of open space therefor).
12. Heating and artificial lighting.
13. Services, installations and ancillary equipment (including services, installations and ancillary equipment for the supply or use of gas or electricity,

and the provision of such arrangements for heating and cooking as are calculated to prevent or control so far as practicable the emission of smoke or noxious gases).

14. Accommodation and ancillary equipment.
15. Access.
16. Prevention of danger and obstruction.

Up until this point there was no universal building control regime in the state. Some corporations, such as Dublin, Cork and Limerick, did have by-laws and some level of inspection and enforcement. But in general, the construction and maintenance on dwellings, whether residential, commercial or leisure, was neither regulated nor subject to any sanction where public safety was put at risk.

Now the Minister for Local Government had the power to design, introduce and enforce a regulatory framework to ensure that all new buildings, including the homes people lived in, would meet certain standards. The regulations would also ensure that builders would face sanctions if they breached these standards, particularly when putting the safety of the residents at risk.

The first draft of the new building regulations was circulated to local authorities in 1969. Following consultation, a revised draft was published in 1976. The main thrust of the proposed regulations was an independent local authority-led inspection and approval system.

Not everyone was happy with the draft. The Construction Industry Federation, representing builders, and the Building Industry Council, representing engineers, architects and surveyors, argued that 'it would present serious problems for the building industry'.[14]

Reports from *The Irish Times* as late as 1978 revealed some of the tensions between the Department of the Environment (the name of the Department of Local Government as of 1977) and the construction sector. The Construction Industry Federation described the proposed mandatory insulation requirement in the regulations as 'entirely unrealistic and bureaucratic'.[15]

Another article in *The Irish Times* said that the Building Industry Council went further, saying that while the draft regulations 'might achieve some improvements in building standards it would be at the expense of a "completely unjustifiable" increase in costs'.[16] They also claimed that the proposed 'control procedures would be beyond the capacity of current local authority staff'.[17]

Both representative bodies submitted detailed comments to the Minister, with the Building Industry Council calling for the current draft regulations to be completely disregarded.

The intensive lobbying paid off. According to one source, 'The Department considered that these objections were well founded and that attempts should be made to produce a new control system based on "self-certification" by the industry.'[18] The draft building regulations were substantially rewritten and then left gathering dust on a shelf in the Department of the Environment.

While industry and government were crafting what would eventually become the state's first comprehensive building control regime, the influential Law Reform Commission entered the debate. In 1977 they published a comprehensive report on *The Law Relating to the Liability of Builders, Vendors and Lessors for the Quality and Fitness of Premises*. The report mapped out the complex and contradictory legal framework covering the building and selling of homes. 'The present law', the report concluded, 'displays an inordinate amount of inconsistencies and injustices.'[19]

The report outlined three key problems in the legal system that shielded builders and sellers of defective homes from liability. The first was the 'unequal bargaining position' between purchaser and seller. The second was a general 'immunity conferred on vendors'. The third was the ability of builders to avail of the same immunity by selling directly or 'using the corporate vehicle, or multiple companies, to evade possible civil liability'.[20] The Law Reform Commission was also concerned that 'in recent years the number of builders who have gone into liquidation is disturbingly high', leaving homeowners carrying the costs of defective building.

To remedy these various problems, the commission proposed a number of reforms, including a statutory register for construction industry professionals, a guarantee scheme funded through an industry levy, and the introduction of individual liability for company directors through which 'the corporate veil should be pierced'.[21]

Following consultation with a range of legal and industry opinion, including the Construction Industry Federation, the Royal Institute of Chartered Surveyors and the Department of the Environment, the Law Reform Commission published their final *Report on Defective Premises*, along with the general scheme of a 'Defective Premises Bill', in 1982. The report and draft legislation proposed introducing a legal 'duty to build premises properly'.[22] The draft bill also sought to place new obligations on vendors and to reform the statute of limitations to apply from the date of discovery of defects rather than the date of sale of property.

This was a far-reaching set of proposals that would have substantially improved protections for homeowners.

It also placed greater responsibility on builders and sellers to ensure properties were built to the appropriate standard.

As with the 1976 draft of the building control regulations, the Law Reform Commission's proposals came up against the powerful interests of the construction industry. Those interests appeared to have greater weight in government than the interests of homeowners, legal professionals or local authority building control officials.

Dr Padraic Kenna's observation in *Housing Law, Rights and Housing Policy* (2011) on the consequence of the 'close connection between certain political personalities and builders' from the 1960s onwards has a particular relevance here and is worth quoting in full:

> A political dynasty had evolved, with the associates of builders, developers and others connected with the construction industry reaching extremely powerful positions. They were able to influence large areas of government policy in a positive or negative way, outside the knowledge or accountability of the electorate. Indeed, it could be said that a political culture and set of networks was established at this time which led to a blatant disregard for the instruments of the State in promoting a rational planning policy in the public interest.[23]

Nowhere was this truer than with regard to building control, an instrument of the state whose purpose was to ensure the buildings we live in, work in and socialise in are safe.

It would take a devastating fire at a nightclub in north Dublin to force the issue of building control back onto the political agenda.

The Stardust

On the night of 14 February 1981, a blaze ripped through the popular Stardust nightclub in Artane, north Dublin. Forty-eight people, mainly teenagers, died. Another 214 were injured, many severely.

According to a team of investigative journalists at TheJournal.ie, 'The Stardust fire was so significant not only because of the scale of the loss of life but also what is seen as the botched attempt by the State to deliver justice.'

In their award-winning six-episode podcast, broadcast in 2019, Sean Murray, Nicky Ryan and Christine Bohan retold the story of that traumatic night, the controversial Tribunal of Inquiry and the families' forty-year campaign for justice.[24]

In response to the fire, the government convened a Tribunal of Inquiry headed by Justice Ronan Keane. His report, published on 14 February 1982, reached a verdict of arson that effectively exonerated the owners of the Stardust nightclub and the authorities of any responsibility for the deaths. The survivors, the families of those who died and the wider community in Artane rejected the tribunal's findings and have, for four decades, campaigned for a fresh inquest. Despite decades of resistance, government finally relented – a fresh inquest is set to commence in 2021.

While the 1981 tribunal report is deeply flawed, it does shine an important light on the lack of any meaningful building control regime. The Department of the Environment comes in for strong criticism for their failure to implement building regulations, despite the minister being empowered to do so in 1963, twenty years before that fatal night in February 1981.

The tribunal's conclusions speak for themselves:

> The Tribunal accepts that the Department of the Environment were obliged to assess, with the greatest care, the difficulties involved in introducing building regulations having the force of law. A delay, however, of just under twenty years in introducing such regulations is wholly unacceptable. The attention of the Department had been drawn on more than one occasion during the decade preceding the fire, to the serious additional work-load being imposed on the Fire Prevention Department of Dublin Corporation because of the absence of such regulations. This, coupled with the knowledge possessed by the Department as to the grave difficulties being experienced by the Corporation in adequately staffing that Department, should have led to this matter being dealt with as one of the greatest urgency. It was deplorable that, far from it being treated as a matter of urgency, the Department official principally concerned with the regulations was transferred to other work for a period of nearly a year.[25]
>
> There is no legally enforceable system of universal application in the Republic of Ireland which requires the fire safety aspect of all new buildings to be considered before permission for their erection is granted. Fire safety control, in the case of new buildings, is exercised only through the legally questionable, and in practice unenforceable, machinery of the Planning Acts, and in such areas as they are enforced, local Bye-laws, which in the case of Dublin are in many respects out of date.[26]

Justice Ronan Keane's recommendation was equally clear:

> The Tribunal accordingly recommends that the Minister for the Environment brings into force Section 86 of the Planning Act, 1963, and makes immediate use of his power under the Section to make building regulations.[27]

In his evidence to the Stardust Tribunal, Aidan McDonald, Principal Officer in the Housing Administration Section of the Department of the Environment, tried to explain to Justice Keane why it was taking so long to produce the building regulations. McDonald cited the administrative burden of creating new organisations in all but six local authorities that had pre-established building control sections; the very substantial and costly staffing requirements that this would involve; the understaffing of the department itself; and the strong opposition of the construction industry to an inspection and approval system.[28]

The failure of government to establish a comprehensive state-wide building control regime placed a significant burden on the fire service. In documents submitted to the Stardust Inquiry, Captain O'Brien of the Dublin Fire Brigade, writing in 1971 to the secretary of the then Department of Local Government, detailed how 75 per cent of his fire-prevention team's time was taken up responding to planning applications.

The lack of a statutory building control regime, the absence of an adequate number of trained inspectors, and the undue burden placed on the fire service were all materially relevant to the scale of the Stardust tragedy. Justice Keane is quite explicit in linking the failure to establish an adequate building control regime and the size of the Stardust fire:

The presence of the wall linings with their low surface spread of flame rating played a major part in this disaster. In addition, the unsatisfactory nature of Exit 2 was a contributing factor in these deaths and injuries. Had the express requirements of the Draft Building Regulations in relation to both of these matters been enforced and observed, the consequences of the disaster might have been significantly diminished.[29]

Within two weeks of the fire, the Department of the Environment published a revised draft of the building control regulations, this time based on the construction industry's preferred self-certification model. Nevertheless, Aidan McDonald of the department told the Stardust Inquiry the regulations wouldn't become law until '1st January 1983 at the earliest'.[30]

In response Justice Keane recommended that given the urgency of preventing future tragedies, the fire-safety elements of the building control regime should be dealt with separately and introduced within three months.[31]

Neither Justice Keane's three-month deadline nor the department's six-month deadline were met. A year and a half after the Stardust Inquiry report was published, the Tánaiste and Minister for the Environment, Labour's Dick Spring, brought a detailed memo to cabinet. The eighty-eight-page document setting out the government's response to the report of the Tribunal of Inquiry into the Stardust fire was finally discussed on 20 December 1983. A cover letter from the Department of the Environment explained that 'The Tánaiste is most anxious that the Memorandum should be submitted and considered by Government as soon as possible.' His frustration stemmed from the fact that the first draft of the memo had been circulated a year earlier, in November 1982.

The memo indicated that 'a Building Control Bill will be introduced at the earliest possible date to provide a new statutory basis for building regulations'.[32] The general scheme had been approved by cabinet the previous May.

The memo tabled by Tánaiste Spring was highly critical of Justice Keane's reprimand to the Department of the Environment for the twenty-year delay in introducing comprehensive building control regulations. It justified this delay by saying that 'There was no public pressure at the time – or indeed subsequently – for the early introduction of building regulations and little or no perception, either publicly or among the many interests concerned with the building industry, that the replacement of the old bye-laws was a matter of urgency, whether for reasons of public safety or otherwise.'[33]

This claim is flatly contradicted by the evidence of Captain O'Brien to the Stardust Inquiry, detailed above; his 1971 correspondence to the then Department of Local Government made clear the need for such regulations on fire-safety grounds.

The claim is also contradicted by a report laid before the Houses of the Oireachtas in 1975 by the then Minister for Local Government, which recommended that 'the sections of the Building Regulations dealing with fire standards and safety should be brought into operation "at the earliest date possible"'.[34]

In a remarkable and revealing passage, the memo states, 'The main argument against the introduction of a new building code related to the extra costs likely to arise from operating it. Generally, the relevance of public health or safety was not a factor in the discussions.'[35]

The memo went on to explain that the department had decided not to proceed with the 1976 building control regulations until they had secured the 'general acceptance' of the building industry. Moreover, the memo argued, 'There is little doubt that if the Minister concerned had proceeded at that stage with the making of the regulations, it would have posed serious difficulties for local authorities operating under the Government's staffing embargoes and for industry in a time of recession.'[36]

Though the country was still deep in recession, the scale of the human tragedy at the Stardust nightclub meant the government had no option but to act. Twenty-one years after the Minister for Local Government had first been given the authority to issue building control regulations, Fine Gael's minister of state in the Department of the Environment, Fergus O'Brien TD, took to his feet in the Dáil chamber to introduce the Building Control Bill 1984.

That it took two full years from the Stardust fire to draft the bill was troubling.

That it took a further decade for the bill to pass all stages of the Oireachtas and to become law was, in light of the number of people who died and were injured in Artane on the night of 14 February 1981, an absolute scandal.

CHAPTER SEVEN

A Long and Torturous Road

Twenty-one years after the Oireachtas passed legislation empowering government to introduce a system for regulating and controlling building standards, the Building Control Bill 1984 was finally introduced.

It took fourteen Dáil and Seanad sittings, over seven years, involving six ministers for the environment and three governments, before the legislation was finally passed. It was signed into law by the President on 21 March 1990, and the regulations took effect in the summer of 1992.

The bill was not particularly long, with twenty-five sections running across twenty-four pages. But it was controversial, and the long and torturous passage of the legislation through the Oireachtas provides an important insight into how and why we ended up with a building control regime that, for Stephanie Meehan, Ciara Holland, Lorraine and Gary Carew, Mark and Aine and Alan, provided zero protection against their defectively built homes.

The 24th Dáil – Minister of State Fergus O'Brien

When the 24th Dáil was elected, Fine Gael and Labour formed a coalition that would last four years, significantly longer than its two immediate predecessors. Labour Party leader Dick Spring was, in 1982, appointed Tánaiste and Minister for the Environment. He was replaced at the Custom House twice during the government's term of office, first by party colleague Liam Kavanagh in 1983 and then by Fine Gael's John Boland in 1986.

While Tánaiste Spring was ultimately responsible for the legislation, the job of steering the Building Control Bill through the Oireachtas was delegated to Minister of State Fergus O'Brien, the Fine Gael TD for Dublin South Central. O'Brien served almost twenty years in the Dáil from his election in 1973 through to 1992. He was also Lord Mayor of Dublin City from 1980 to 1981 and was serving in that office when the Stardust fire took place.

In his opening remarks during the Second Stage debate in the Dáil, he referenced Justice Keane's Tribunal findings, 'that there had been a 20 year delay in making building regulations'.[1] Nonetheless, he explained his predecessor's failure to act on Section 86 of the Local Government Act of 1963, saying that 'It is no part of my purpose here to defend what did – or did not happen – over the years but I feel that I should point out that the power conferred on the Minister in 1963 was an enabling one and that it did not impose an obligation on the Minister to make building regulations by any particular date, or indeed at all.'[2]

Echoing the language in Dick Spring's 1983 cabinet memo on the Stardust Inquiry report, he said, 'there was no public pressure at the time … either publicly or among the many interests concerned with the building industry' to introduce building regulations.[3] While he confirmed that the first draft of the regulations had been completed in 1965, it was decided not to proceed until consultation with the building industry had secured 'their general acceptance'.[4]

The minister of state, reinforcing the views of both the Construction Industry Federation and the Building Industry Council in their submissions to that consultation, argued that 'There is little doubt that if regulations had been made at that stage they would have posed serious difficulties not only for industry but also local authorities.'[5]

The consequences would, again in language similar to the industry lobbies of the 1970s, 'create costly delays in getting construction projects underway and seriously affect efficiency and employment in industry'.[6]

O'Brien then outlined a short history of the evolution of the content of the bill before the Dáil.

Earlier drafts sought to apply a local authority-led inspection regime, similar to but stronger than that in existence under the corporations' by-laws. Such an approach would require 'the recruitment of a substantial number of suitably qualified staff in each local authority area', which would impose 'a substantial financial burden on local authorities'.[7] Following submissions from the construction industry during the 1970s, the minister explained, 'an alternative system of control, based on certification by the industry itself was being developed'.[8]

The shift from a local authority-led independent inspection regime to a construction industry-led self-certification system was knocked off course by the recommendations of the Keane Tribunal into the Stardust fire. Minister of State

O'Brien informed the Dáil, 'The tribunal considered that it would be undesirable to rely solely on a certification system where fire safety is concerned.'[9] And so Section 6 of the bill was amended to take account of this.

Section 6 included a requirement for developers to apply to the local authority for a 'fire safety certificate' which when issued would confirm that 'the building concerned will, in the authority's opinion, comply with specified fire parts of the regulations'.[10]

Nevertheless, the minister of state went on to clarify that 'building control authorities will not be required to carry out inspections to ensure compliance with the regulations'. He added, 'therefore, it will be a matter for the designers and builders to ensure that the work is carried out in accordance with the regulations', including fire-safety regulations.[11]

The bill also included a number of exemptions from the certification regime, including state, semi-state and local authority buildings, as well as low-rise housing and small extensions. In what he termed 'the essence of the system' proposed in the bill, the minister of state said that 'it will not involve building control authorities in a scrutiny of, or in giving approval for, individual projects'.[12] While local authorities 'will have the power to carry out random checks and inspections on buildings', he stressed that 'they will not be under any duty to ensure that buildings erected comply with the requirements of the regulations'.[13] This, he made clear, would be the responsibility of the designers and builders.

The first speaker in the debate from the opposition was the Fianna Fáil Galway West TD, Bobby Molloy. Not to be outdone by the minister of state's championing the interests of the construction industry, Molloy expressed 'concern' at the 'lack of consultation' with that sector prior to the publication of the bill.[14]

Despite the legislation having been in gestation since its first draft in 1965, the Fianna Fáil TD urged caution, 'that in our haste we do not impose something on the construction industry which is unworkable'.[15] He called for a 'gradual' introduction of any new regulations and questioned the rationale for sanctions whereby 'individuals who have been working in the industry and doing their best … feel that they are unavoidably being placed in a semi-criminal position, having to prove their innocence' if anything goes wrong.[16]

Deputy Molloy was particularly exercised that liability could fall on 'individual members such as directors, managers or secretaries who would be subject to fines of up to £10,000 and two years in prison'.[17] In what would turn out to be a prescient question, he asked who would have responsibility for faults that 'may not appear in a building for 20 years'.[18]

Fianna Fáil's verdict on the bill was very straightforward. It would 'have the effect of increasing costs considerably' and amounted to 'a major burden being added to an industry already on its knees'.[19] As a result, Deputy Molloy concluded, 'I don't not think the Bill in its present form should be enacted.'[20]

In what can only be described as Orwellian doublespeak, Deputy Molloy told the Dáil that 'There is an urgency about the introduction of uniform regulations but there is a need to proceed with caution so that we do not impose something on the industry that will cause it major problems.'[21]

The fifth speaker in the debate that evening was the Labour TD for Dublin South West, Mervyn Taylor. He was the first to broaden the debate beyond the needs of industry and to include the relevance of building control for the 'member of the public who buys a house, or the businessman who acquires or has built for him a factory'.[22] For Taylor the purpose of the bill was to ensure that the buyer was 'guaranteed that he gets what he paid for … a properly built house … [or] a factory that is usable and suitable for its purpose'.[23] He described the bill as 'a disappointment' as it 'is not directed towards increasing any rights, powers or remedies to a person who buys a new house or factory that is defective in some way'.[24]

In another prescient moment in the debate, the Labour TD acknowledged that the bill did allow for legal sanctions for failure to comply with the regulations, including fines and imprisonment, but 'our experience has shown us that prosecutions for breaches of planning regulations and bye-law approvals in the past have not resulted in imprisonment or in substantial fines being imposed, although there have been some pretty appalling things done'.[25]

At the centre of Deputy Taylor's criticism of the bill was the need to place a 'duty to build properly' as recommended in the 1982 Law Reform Commission report on defective premises. Such a duty would ensure that the person 'who undertakes the work is responsible for damages if he fails to do the work properly'.[26] This liability, argued Taylor, should not just apply to the initial purchaser of the property 'but to any unfortunate person who is unlucky enough to acquire or buy it if the defect does not show up for many years'.[27]

Taylor's conclusion was that the purchaser of a defective building 'is getting no protection from the Building Control Bill'.[28] He was particularly concerned about cases where the builder responsible for the defects 'has gone into liquidation'.

The Labour TD urged the minister of state to make two key amendments to the bill. The first was that where a builder does not comply with the regulations, they should be responsible for rectifying the defects by way of compensation. The second was that local authorities should have a legal obligation to ensure compliance.[29]

During the debate, the only other contributor to focus on the need for a stronger building control regime was Dublin North West Workers' Party TD Proinsias De Rossa. Speaking on Tuesday 5 June, the second day of the debate, he challenged the 'vested interests in the building industry' and said, 'it is the duty of this House to enact laws that will regulate and set high standards for the good of the community'.[30]

De Rossa also stressed that from the consumer's point of view the new system of control must ensure that they will have the right of redress in the event of negligence.[31] For emphasis, he declared, 'If negligence is proved, the guilty party must pay.'[32]

On Tuesday, 19 June, Fergus O'Brien, Minister of State at the Department of the Environment, responded to the deputies who had participated in the Second Stage debate. He reminded Fianna Fáil's Bobby Molloy that 'extensive consultations with representatives of industry' had taken place since 1976, and 'particularly since 1981'.[33] To all those deputies concerned with the impact of the proposed regime on industry, the minister of state emphasised, 'It was in fact industry that requested this particular system [self-certification] rather than an approval system [by local authorities] as a means of reducing costs and eliminating long and unnecessary delays.'[34]

Nowhere in his comments did O'Brien respond to any of Mervyn Taylor's concerns about consumer protection or compensation. Similarly, the minister of state ignored the central contributions of Proinsias De Rossa.

Fergus O'Brien concluded the debate by saying it was 'important that the Bill proceed as quickly as possible', as he didn't 'want the momentum to drop'.[35] The minister's hope was to be dashed, however, as it would be two years before the bill progressed to the Seanad, and a full four and a half years before it returned to the Dáil.

The lengthy delay in the passage of the legislation was marked by another tragedy: when two people lost their lives in a gas explosion in Raglan House on Serpentine Avenue, Dublin, on 1 January 1987. Noelle and Michael Murphy, both in their 40s, died when the building collapsed. Noelle was a radiographer in Crumlin Children's Hospital and her husband was an outside broadcaster for RTÉ.

The severity of the explosion led to the passing of the Local Government (Multi-Storey Buildings) Act in 1988. The legislation sought to put in place a risk assessment for mid-rise apartment blocks that may have methane gas problems. During the course of a number of Dáil debates preceding this new bill, TDs and senators urged government to reintroduce the Building Control Bill for completion.

Ger Connolly, TD for Laois–Offaly and Minister of State at the Department of the Environment, told TDs during an adjournment debate on the Raglan House explosion on 25 November that 'I want to emphasise again the importance of the building regulations', and he assured deputies that 'these regulations will be brought before the House as soon as possible'.

In the general election of February 1987, Fianna Fáil were returned to power, appointing Pádraig Flynn TD as Minister for the Environment. Despite the fact that the

Raglan House tragedy placed building control back on the political agenda, the minister did not return to the House with the Building Control Bill for almost a year and a half.

Flynn was an experienced politician and cabinet member. First elected to the Mayo West constituency in 1977, he retained his seat until 1993, when he was appointed by Taoiseach Albert Reynolds to the European Commission. A loyal supporter of Charles Haughey in the 1979 Fianna Fáil leadership contest, he was rewarded by being appointed Minister of State for Transport in that year. Before his promotion to the Custom House in 1987, he also served as Minister for the Gaeltacht and then Minister for Trade.

He was one of a number of senior Fianna Fáil politicians whose close relationship with developers, including Tom Gilmartin, was to prove very profitable. Author Frank Connolly, in his bestselling *Tom Gilmartin: The Man who Brought Down a Taoiseach and Exposed the Greed and Corruption at the Heart of Irish Politics* (2015), estimates that Flynn received payments from developers in excess of £155,000 between 1987 and 1993.

The 25th Dáil – Minister Pádraig Flynn

The first of the five committee meetings dealing with the Building Control Bill took place in December 1988. With just four members contributing – Minister Pádraig Flynn for the Fianna Fáil government, Deputies Ruairi Quinn and Mervyn Taylor for Labour and Proinsias De Rossa for the Workers' Party – it was a rather subdued affair. The committee dealt with eleven relatively technical amendments, three from Labour and eight from government. Significantly, no deputy from Fine Gael, then the largest opposition party, participated in the meeting.

When the committee reconvened on 15 February 1989, it was a much livelier session. Minister Flynn tabled a new version of the controversial Section 6, dealing with self-certification. Deputy De Rossa tabled an amendment that would have required local authorities to undertake all certification. The Workers' Party were opposed to what they called 'the privatisation of building control'. De Rossa argued that 'There are no good grounds for believing that self-certification is in the interests of people.'[36]

Minister Flynn was clear in his opposition to the Workers' Party amendment, accusing De Rossa and his Workers' Party colleague Pat McCartan of showing 'a strong anti-construction industry bias' during the discussion.[37]

Surprisingly the Labour Party were also not supporting the Workers' Party amendment. Despite Deputy Taylor taking a critical approach to his own government's Bill at Second Stage back in 1984, the party's new Environment spokesperson, Ruairi Quinn, told the committee that 'I have no difficulty with the principal of self-certification.'[38]

The committee session was taking place a day after the eighth anniversary of the Stardust tragedy. Quinn accused De Rossa of wanting to 'preserve' the local authority approval system that had been in place at the time of the fire. The Labour spokesperson's argument was that 'the real tragedy is that building [the nightclub] was not designed or executed by a properly qualified professional'.[39]

While partially true, Deputy Quinn's position ignored the very strong view of Justice Keane that the failure to have an independent building control and fire certification regime added to an under-resourcing of the Dublin Fire Brigade, which was also key to understanding the tragedy.

In the lengthy and heated exchange that followed between the two opposition spokespersons, the Workers' Party deputies made the case for an independent and resourced local authority-led inspection regime. In response the Labour Party urged that self-certification be combined with severe sanctions and proper enforcement.[40]

In the end the Workers' Party–Labour Party disagreement was a sideshow, since the government had the numbers to defeat De Rossa's amendment.

As the committee session drew to a close, and clearly having lost his patience with De Rossa and McCartan, Minister Flynn made one final assault on their alternative proposal for a local authority-led approval system. 'They are saying that without that kind of local authority approval system building defects will not be detected,' the minister opined.

The Workers' Party amendment wouldn't be voted on for nine months, as the June 1989 general election intervened, returning another Fianna Fáil government – this time in coalition with the recently formed Progressive Democrats.

The 26th Dáil – Minister for the Environment Pádraig Flynn

Committee Stage of the Building Control Bill was finally completed in a marathon session on 29 November 1989. In contrast to the previous meetings, Fine Gael played a significant part in proceedings through their Dublin South TD Alan Shatter. Committee dealt with fourteen separate amendments to the government's own amended Section 6, none of which were accepted.

Deputy Shatter's main contributions to the debate focused on two key areas. He wanted to 'ensure that the individuals involved in the designing and construction of the building are not the people who do the necessary certification'.[41] In addition he wanted local authorities to have a duty to 'ensure that the certificate of compliance complies with the requirements of the Act'.[42]

Minister Flynn rejected what he termed 'third party certification' on the grounds that it would 'impose a layer of cost similar to that pertaining to the local authority system' and that it would result in project delays, particularly for complex projects.

The new Workers' Party Environment spokesperson, Eamon Gilmore TD, continued his party's strident opposition to self-certification. 'The principal being enshrined in this section is very dangerous,' he said. 'It will expose people who are buying homes to buying products which are substandard against which they will have no comeback.'[43]

Again the minister rejected the opposition's arguments, claiming that builders and developers would 'only be able to continue in business as long as they have good quality work as their trade mark'.[44] Flynn was adamant that he did 'not believe that anything in this Bill will expose home buyers to the possibility of buying a sub-standard building'.[45]

As the meeting ground on, Minister Flynn and Deputy Gilmore continued to tussle over the level of protection for the home buyer where the property was to prove defective. The minister was insistent that the system as proposed incentivised both the builder and architect-certifier to comply with the building regulations, to ensure their good reputations.

Gilmore asked, 'Suppose there was a rogue builder and architect, that the certificate of compliance does not hold up and the defect in the building does not emerge until I happen to buy it, what comeback would I have?'[46]

In response Flynn said, 'I cannot for the life of me understand the Deputy's preoccupation with rogue builders, certifiers and architects', to which Gilmore shot back, 'I come across a lot of them.'[47]

In one of the debate's most revealing remarks, Minister Flynn stated, 'If Deputy Gilmore buys a building without having put in place some checks ... then he is the one who is being negligent in protecting his own investment.'[48]

The substantive debate was over. The government had the numbers, and once the opposition amendments to the government's revised Section 6 were disposed of, the committee proceeded with the remainder of the technical amendments. Two weeks later, on Wednesday 13 December, the report and final stages of the bill were completed in the Dáil. It was then sent to the Seanad, where its passage was swift, concluding on 15 March 1990.

The Building Control Act 1990 was now law. All that remained was for the officials from the Department of the Environment, in consultation with industry, to draft up the technical building regulations.

Finalising the regulations took a further year. They were published in twelve volumes in December 1991 and took effect the following June. Speaking at their launch, the newly appointed Minister for the Environment, Rory O'Hanlon, was reported in *The Irish Times* as saying, 'the safety of the building environment was of crucial importance because "we spend most of our lives in buildings of one sort or another"'.[49]

The minister was satisfied that the 'vast majority' of construction industry professionals would comply with the new rules.[50] However, according to *The Irish Times*, 'local authority building control officers have expressed concern that [the new regime] will give carte blanche to "rogue builders"'.[51]

After thirty years, the state finally had a regulatory regime for the construction and maintenance of buildings. The purpose of the regime was to ensure that buildings were built properly, to clear standards and were safe. The regulations also included an enforcement regime to ensure that were the rules broken those responsible would be held to account.

With the economy about to emerge from recession and commence the biggest building boom in the history of the state, the Building Control Act of 1990 was to be tested in the most extreme of circumstances.

CHAPTER EIGHT

What Happens When ...?

Minister for the Environment Pádraig Flynn did not believe the opposition's contention 'that without [a] local authority approval system building defects will not be detected'. He argued strongly that self-certification would ensure that building defects would be discovered, even though there was no obligation on local authorities to inspect individual developments. Little did he know how wrong he would be, and how right his opponents were to warn of the dangers of self-certification.

The Mayo West TD seemed incredulous when Eamon Gilmore raised the prospect of 'rogue builders and architects' breaking the rules and building defective homes: 'I cannot for the life of me understand the Deputy's preoccupation with rogue builders, certifiers and architects.' While Gilmore may have been in a minority of TDs who, as he said in riposte to the minister, had 'come across a lot of them', the Celtic Tiger would change all of that.

If you want to know what happens when you privatise building control, the construction boom from 1995 to 2008 provides an uncomfortable, and at times harmful, lesson in why self-certification was the wrong choice.

Boom

In 1990, the year the Building Control Bill was finally passed into law, the economy was in a deep recession. Less than 100,000 people were employed in construction. Just 19,539 new homes were built that year – one of the lowest out-turns in over a decade. The total value of mortgage lending that year was €6.5 million.

Within a decade the construction sector had been transformed and became the turbo-charged engine of the second phase of the Celtic Tiger economic boom. House completions rose to 30,575 in 1995 and continued to rise to 49,812 in 2000. In every year that followed, a new historic record was reached. In 2005 there were 85,419 new home completions.

But the record was set the following year with an astonishing 88,419 new houses and apartments built. That's an average of 242 new homes completed every single day.

With all that building, the number of people employed directly and indirectly in the construction industry soared. In 2007 there were an estimated 270,000 people working in construction, with a further 100,000 employed indirectly. In 2006, 13.4 per cent of all workers in Ireland were in construction, almost twice the EU average.

More dramatic than the increase in construction employment or output was the astounding rise in house prices. From 1997 to 2005 house prices increased by almost 200 per cent. Nearly every single year from 1995 to 2006 saw double-digit house-price inflation. In 2004 alone, prices increased by 20 per cent.

In 1994, an average house in Dublin would cost you €81,000. By 1998 the same property was worth €160,000.

By 2004 the value had skyrocketed to €311,000. Outside of Dublin, prices rose just as dramatically, from €66,000 in 1994 to €116,000 in 1998 and to €228,000 in 2004. These dramatic increases in property values were fuelled by low-cost easy-access credit, 100 per cent mortgages, sub-prime lending to modest-income working families and government-backed tax breaks for buy-to-let landlords.[1]

The ever-growing volume of mortgage credit was truly staggering, increasing almost fivefold by 2000 to €32 million. By 2005 total outstanding mortgage debt rose to €94 million. In 2007 it reached its high point at a total of €1.23 billion.

Home building was big money. The more you could build, the more you could make. The faster you built and sold, the quicker you could move on to the next development. The demand for labour was so great and the money so attractive, young builders were walking off apprenticeships and onto sites with less than adequate training.

If ever there was an environment that incentivised cutting corners to get a job done, this was it. And while 'rogue builders' may have been a minority, they were building more and more properties, at even greater speed, for ever growing profits. In the absence of an independent inspection regime, or a requirement for local authorities to inspect even a representative portion of developments under construction, the chances of significant building defects going undetected was high.

And despite Minister Flynn's conviction that developers, builders and architects would keep to the rules to maintain their good trading name, a lot of defective buildings were built, sold and occupied. Their new owners, delighted and relieved to have the security of owning their own home, had no idea that they were living in non-compliant and, in some cases, potentially dangerous buildings.

Defects – Pyrite

The first significant Celtic Tiger latent defect issue that came to light was pyrite. This invisible mineral substance is found in certain kinds of rock often used as hardcore in building foundations, including in residential developments. In certain conditions pyrite can swell and cause damage to foundations.

In 2005 homeowners in a number of estates in Fingal County Council noticed cracking in the internal and external walls of their homes. Initial attempts to plaster over what were – wrongly – considered settling cracks failed to address the problem.[2] Between 2005 and 2007 investigations by Ballymun Regeneration Company and the insurers HomeBond and Premier Guarantee discovered pyrite in a number of the developments. While initially the two building defects insurance providers covered the cost of remediation works, this changed in 2011 when HomeBond, the industry-led insurance product managed by the Irish Home Builders Association, refused to fund any future works.[3]

A Pyrite Action Group, made up of homeowners living in properties damaged by pyrite, was formed to campaign for government action. In the ensuing public and political storm, the then Minister for the Environment, Phil Hogan, set up an Independent Pyrite Panel in September 2011. Its job was to establish the extent of the problem and make recommendations to government for action.

The panel's report was published the following June. It identified seventy-four housing estates, spread across

Fingal, Meath, Kildare, Offaly and Dublin City, affected by pyrite. While some of the 12,250 homes they identified had been remediated, there were as many as 10,300 at risk from potential structural defects caused by pyrite.[4] The report was also clear in stating that neither government nor homeowners should have to pay for the remediation of affected properties. They proposed the establishment of a Pyrite Resolution Board funded through a levy on the quarrying and construction sectors.

In March 2013 Minister Hogan announced his intention to establish a €50 million resolution fund financed through levy on the construction, quarrying and insurance industries. An industry-led company, Pyremco, was registered with the Companies Registration Office that month, with an address at the headquarters of the Construction Industry Federation. Pyremco was to be the vehicle that would undertake remediation work for qualifying homeowners.

Nevertheless, as the legislation to underpin the scheme was being finalised, one of the sectors contributing to the scheme threatened legal action against the state. Rather than face down the industry lobby, the government abandoned the key recommendation of the Pyrite Panel's report that those responsible should cover the costs of fixing defective homes. When the Pyrite Resolution Bill 2013 was introduced in the Oireachtas in December, the fund had been reduced to just €10 million, and it was funded by the taxpayer.

During the passage of the legislation, Minister Hogan told the Oireachtas that attempts to get the industry to agree to a voluntary scheme were unsuccessful. He went on to say that the consequent decision to impose a levy on the industry hit 'legal and constitutional' problems, making the scheme 'impossible to implement'. So, with the industry off the hook, the taxpayer would have to foot the bill.

The Pyrite Resolution Board, located within the Housing Agency, was established that year; by 2014 it was on a statutory footing and receiving applications for remediation. To date it has received 2,592 applications for funding to address structural damage; by the end of 2019, it remediated 1,890 of these. A further 200 are expected to be completed in 2020, and 300 more in 2021. Homes in County Limerick were added to the scheme in 2020.

While the Independent Pyrite Panel initially estimated the cost of remediation per home at €45,000, the actual average cost was closer to €65,000. Since 2014 the state has spent €158.8 million, including €20 million allocated for 2021. This figure does not include the cost to local authorities, including Dublin City Council and Fingal County Council, for the remediation of social housing affected by pyrite.

It will be some years before we know the total number of properties remediated and the final cost to the taxpayer. There are also an even greater number of properties in estates affected by pyrite that, because they have not yet experienced any pyrite-related structural defects, are not eligible for remediation. Despite this, the value of their homes has fallen dramatically and many owners are stranded in negative equity.

Defective Concrete Blocks

The Pyrite Resolution Board dealt in the main with properties where pyrite was found in the building's foundations. In 2008 homeowners and council tenants in Counties Mayo and Donegal started to experience damage to their properties that originated from within the concrete building blocks.

Initial tests discovered pyrite in the blocks in Mayo and another substance known as mica in the blocks in Donegal. The scale and cost of remediating the affected properties would be much more substantial than the cost of remediating pyrite in foundations, as it would require either replacing the entire outer leaf of the building, or full demolition and rebuilding of the property.

In a position that was hard to reconcile with his establishment of the pyrite remediation scheme, Minister for the Environment Phil Hogan told Donegal TD Pádraig Mac Lochlainn in a parliamentary question response on 27 May 2014 that, with respect to homeowners with defective concrete blocks, such 'building defects are matters for resolution between the contracting parties, i.e. the homeowner, the builder, the manufacturer, supplier, quarry owner and/or their respective solicitors'.

The minister suggested that affected homeowners should seek redress through the courts. Given that the Pyrite Resolution Board was established because it was impossible for owners to successfully pursue the cost of remediation through the courts, Minister Hogan's advice provoked considerable anger.

Mica and pyrite action groups were set up in both counties to pressurise government to provide support for those affected. In 2015 the minister of state with responsibility for the issue, Fine Gael's Paudie Coffey, commissioned a technical report. This, in turn, led to the establishment of an Expert Panel on Concrete Blocks in April 2016, whose report on the issue was published in June 2017. The report concluded that up to 4,800 private and council properties were affected by mica in Donegal and a further 345 properties were affected by pyrite in Mayo.

Persistent campaigning by those affected eventually led to a breakthrough with the creation of a new local authority-administered remediation scheme announced in 2020, with funding of €20 million for 2021. Unlike the Housing Agency pyrite scheme, homeowners in Counties Donegal and Mayo were expected to pay for 10 per cent of the remediation costs.

The scheme covered the costs of either replacing the outer leaf of the home up to a maximum of €75,000, or full demolition and rebuild costs up to a maximum of €247,500. However, applicants would have to pay up front for an engineer's survey, which could cost as much as €7,000. There would also be no financial support for planning fees, internal fittings or the cost of renting while works were carried out.

To date, no funding has been drawn down, though some works have started. In March 2021, seventy-seven applications had been received by Mayo County Council and 234 by Donegal County Council. By June the number in Donegal had increased to 354, with 225 approvals.

As more applicants joined the scheme, concern over the adequacy of the grant level was being expressed, with some homeowners estimating that they would be liable for up to 30 per cent of the full costs of remediation.

Tom McFeely – Priory Hall and Áras na Cluaine

As detailed earlier, 187 apartments in Priory Hall were built by developer Tom McFeely's Coalport company. The fire-safety defects were so bad that, in 2011, all 256 residents had to be evacuated. After a long, hard and traumatic campaign, an agreement was finally reached between homeowners, banks and government that saw the state take responsibility for completely remediating the entire development. Owner-occupiers were able to walk away debt free and secure new mortgages for new homes. Buy-to-let landlords were given a mortgage holiday until the works were done. Social housing tenants had already been rehoused after their evacuation by Dublin City Council in 2009.

The remediation works were eventually finished in 2021, and the new apartments in the renamed New Priory estate went on the market retailing at €260,000. The cost of rebuilding Priory Hall was €45 million. With up to €30 million to be recouped from the sale of the apartments, the final net cost to the state will be in the region of €20 million.

Priory Hall wasn't the only development with latent defects built by Tom McFeely's Coalport. Áras na Cluaine is a 198-unit apartment complex on the edge of Clondalkin Village, Dublin 22. From 2010 residents were experiencing a range of problems in the development. Some were related to poor-quality maintenance, such as the estate's electronic gate being broken and rubbish not being collected. However, more serious fire-safety issues led to an inspection by the Dublin Fire Brigade in 2010. Failure by Coalport to address the defects led to Dublin City Council taking legal proceedings against McFeely's company.

A court order for evacuation was eventually avoided, as the essential fire-safety work on the premises was completed by Coalport. Dublin City Council deemed the apartments fire-safety compliant in March 2011.[5] A new management company was formed, and the residents, now in charge of running the development, started the slow process of addressing the complex's other issues. McFeely had also run up a significant bill of unpaid management fees for the apartments of which he retained ownership; this caused further financial problems for the cash-strapped owners' management company.

The development came to the attention of the media again in 2015, when Storm Frank destroyed a significant section of the complex's rooftop – another legacy of the poor-quality work from Coalport that was left to the owners to finance and fix.[6]

Bernard McNamara – Longboat Quay

One of the Celtic Tiger's most successful developers, Bernard McNamara, was also caught up in a defects scandal. Completed in 2006, Longboat Quay, located on the south side of the River Liffey, is a 298-unit apartment complex. It was a mixture of social, affordable and private homes, with thirty-seven units owned by the Dublin Docklands Development Authority.

McNamara was once a Fianna Fáil elected representative, serving two terms on Clare County Council. His 1981 general election run proved unsuccessful, leading him to focus on building his property empire.

The scale of McNamara's property acquisitions, at its apex, was eyewatering. Frank McDonald and Kathy Sheridan, in their book *The Builders* (2008), list land purchases including the Ringsend Glass Bottle Site in Dublin for €412 million. The *Irish Times* journalists note that in 2006, Belltrap, the parent company used by McNamara and his co-developer Jerry O'Reilly, paid the two directors a combined dividend of €9.3 million in addition to a €4 million payment on deferred profits for 2005.

In 2012 he went bust and declared bankruptcy in the UK. It was reported that he had debts exceeding €1.2 billion.[7]

In early 2015 the residents of McNamara's Longboat Quay were called to a management company meeting and informed that the building had significant fire-safety and structural defects. They were told that the estimated cost per home could be as much as €20,000. Protracted negotiations between the Dublin Docklands Development Authority, the owners' management company and the receiver (appointed after McNamara went into liquidation) dragged on for two years. The dispute was over who would pay the estimated €3.88 million bill to make the building safe.

A draft agreement was proposed, splitting the cost three ways, with Dublin City Council – who had assumed responsibility for the now wound-down Dublin Docklands Development Authority – paying €2.25 million, the receiver covering €250,000 and homeowners left shelling out €1.2 million.

Initially, McNamara rejected claims that the building was defective. In December 2015 he wrote to the residents individually, saying that 'I am confident in LBQ structural build. It has three hour rated concrete walls and floors ... with no possibility of fire or smoke penetration between apartments or corridors and apartments.'[8]

While at one stage McNamara was threatening legal action, he then shifted tack and offered to remediate the building at cost. Now out of bankruptcy and back in Dublin, he was keen to ensure his reputation was not further damaged.[9]

A deal was finally reached in December 2016 that would see Dublin City Council pay €1.85 million and the receiver a further €1.25 million. While the residents would not be charged for the work, the taxpayer was left footing a bill of €3.1 million to allow McNamara's company, Gendsong, to remediate the defects.

Bernard McNamara is now back where he started: involved in large-scale residential developments. His company, Cinamol, was granted planning permission for a build-to-rent strategic housing development of 110 units in April 2019 located in Swords, County Dublin.[10] He also has interests in developments in Dublin City Centre and Drogheda.

Newlyn Developments Ltd – Foxford Court

Another development where the original builder played a role in the eventual remediation was Foxford Court in Lucan, County Dublin. Built as an affordable housing scheme in 2004, it was a partnership between South Dublin County Council, who provided the land and mortgage finance, and Newlyn Developments Ltd.

Unlike McNamara and McFeely, the directors of Newlyn never went into liquidation. With €20 million of debt transferred to NAMA, they traded at a significant loss in the early years of the post-Celtic Tiger crash. Company directors Christy Dowling, George McGary and Robert Kehoe collectively received €1.9 million in payments and pensions in 2007 following a bumper year of sales in 2006 of €70 million.[11]

In November 2012 residents living in the fifty-two-unit Lucan apartment and duplex development discovered no separation between party walls. They could literally shake hands between two units, underneath the wall, when they lifted their floorboards.[12] An inspection of three properties in February 2013 funded by the owners' management company revealed further defects, including an absence of fire stopping.

When the defects were brought to the attention of South Dublin County Council, they moved to remediate their own three units in the complex but washed their hands of any responsibility for the private homes. Newlyn Developments Ltd were also initially unwilling to get involved, not returning emails sent on behalf of the owners to engage in finding a resolution.

Faced with potential bills of up to €10,000 per unit, residents were divided over what to do next. Legal advice to the owners made clear that litigation would be costly and risky. Frustrated with the lack of progress, the owners who initially discovered the defects went public in March 2013. Fearful of damage to their reputations, South Dublin County Council and Newlyn Developments Ltd met and hammered out an agreement, the details of which were never made public.

In October 2013 the *Dublin Gazette* newspaper reported that a deal had finally been struck.[13] Costs would be split three ways between the council, Newlyn and residents. While the final total cost of the works, or the breakdown of how much each party was to pay, was never revealed, it was confirmed that all units would require some work. Unlike Bernard McNamara, Newlyn did contribute to the cost, but once again the taxpayer was left picking up a significant part of the tab.

Paddy Byrne – Millfield Manor

While some of the fire-safety defects in Celtic Tiger-era developments would be classified as constituting a 'threat to property' others definitely were a 'threat to life'.

In March 2015 a fire ripped through a terrace of six houses in Millfield Manor, Newbridge, County Kildare. The timber frame construction used in the buildings was meant to provide an hour-long fire break between each dwelling. The blaze burnt all six homes to the ground in just twenty-five minutes.

The ninety-house development was built by Barrack Construction between 2006 and 2009. It is estimated that repairs to homes throughout the estate affected by similar defects could cost as much as €35,000 each.[14]

In September 2015 the then Minister for the Environment, Alan Kelly, commissioned a report into the use of timber frame construction, with the Millfield Manor fire to be used as a case study. It would be two years before the full report, including the fire-safety assessment of Millfield Manor, would be published. When it was, residents described it as a 'whitewash', as it identified only 'moderate' risk of fire in the estate.[15]

The Director of Barrack Homes, Paddy Byrne, was and continues to be a controversial figure. With debts of €100 million, including €25 million held by NAMA, the builder filed for bankruptcy in Britain in 2011. According to the *Irish Mail on Sunday*, he was one of only two Irish developers to have had his bankruptcy extended from one year to ten years, in 2013. A report by Michael O'Farrell in that paper detailed how the UK Insolvency Service discovered that Byrne had wrongly sought to conceal funds by transferring €500,000 to his ex-wife and a further €500,000 to his niece.[16]

In 2012 Paddy Byrne formed a new company, Victoria Homes, with his sister, Joan Byrne, listed as director, albeit under her married name Joan Murphy.[17] By 2019 Victoria Homes was involved in more than twenty-four separate developments, including a proposed 1,500-unit development on the Glenamuck Road in Sandyford, County Dublin.[18]

Nonetheless, Byrne was in debt trouble again when, in 2020, one of Victoria Homes' funders, the Lotus Investment Group, appointed receivers to some of the company's assets.[19] Lotus has loaned over €70 million to Victoria Homes. Byrne told the *Irish Independent* that despite the move by Lotus, the company was in a 'strong financial and equity position'.[20]

South Dublin County Council and Gama – Balgaddy

Not all of the high-profile latent defects cases are private developments. On the border of Clondalkin and Lucan are three social housing estates – Meile an Rí, Tor an Rí and Buirg an Rí – collectively known as Balgaddy. Designed by three separate architect teams – Seán Harrington, O'Mahony Pike and the South Dublin County Council's Architects Department – the estate is made up of over 400 houses, duplexes and apartments.

Its unusual design has generated much comment; it is a significant break from the traditional suburban terraced council housing estate dominant throughout the country. Harrington's eighty-three-unit, Tor an Rí, won a Royal Institute of Irish Architects Silver Medal in 2006.

While its architectural style was certainly innovative, the estate had all the hallmarks of poor urban planning, with no shops, playing facilities or public transport to the main population centres – the Lucan, Clondalkin or Tallaght villages.

Even before Balgaddy's new residents started to move in, the development was gripped by controversy. The contractor, Turkish building company Gama Construction, was underpaying and overworking its Turkish workforce. Industrial action halted works in the estate for weeks and was the subject of legal action in Ireland and Turkey.

The exploitation of workers was only the first of many problems to beset the estate. Not long after tenants moved in, issues of damp, poor ventilation and faulty heating systems were being reported to the council.

While South Dublin County Council maintained the majority of the development, two blocks of apartments in Meile an Rí Drive were managed by the approved housing body, Cara Housing. In 2009 Cara was concerned with the high number of maintenance requests and their cost in the twenty-four apartments. It commissioned Thorntons Chartered Surveyors to inspect the building. The fifty-one-page confidential report revealed a litany of structural defects in the walls and roofs. The report confirmed that some of those defects made the apartments prone to mould and damp.

Cara Housing commissioned a second survey in 2010 from EML Architects. The confidential report uncovered significant structural defects, breaches of building regulations and poor-quality construction work causing 'dilapidation'.

The escalating costs of building maintenance became so great that Cara Housing eventually had to hand the management of Meile an Rí Drive back to the council in 2010. In one case prior to the return of the properties to South Dublin County Council, defective roof construction caused the collapse of an entire ceiling in one of the third-floor apartments.

Meanwhile tenants from all three Balgaddy estates were complaining about mould, damp and defective heating systems. Frustrated with the refusal of the council to acknowledge the depth of the problem, they sought support from local councillors, solicitors and the media.

While South Dublin County Council was pursuing Gama through court arbitration to both complete repairs and fund others to do so, their public position was that the development had been 'supervised on site by well-regarded architectural consultants' and that 'Council clerks of works monitored the schemes during construction and compliances were signed by the consultant architects Murray O'Laoghaire and Sean Harrington Architects'.[21]

A campaign, led by the residents' Balgaddy Working Together group, secured support from the South Dublin County Partnership to fund a wider study of the development. In the summer of 2011 Buckeridge Forristal Partnership Consulting Engineers carried out a survey of thirty-nine properties. Their report, which ran into hundreds of pages, found problems including damp and mould, roof leaks, faulty plumbing, heating and electrics, and defective windows.

In a written response to the three inspection reports provided to councillors in November 2011, South Dublin County Council said many of the issues had never been reported to their maintenance department and those that had were now addressed or in the process of being addressed. The council assured 'residents, local Councillors and Dáil representatives that all works required will be completed through a systematic inspection and remedial works programme'.[22]

The following February, Dublin Mid-West Sinn Féin published a detailed report based on a survey of residents in Balgaddy.[23] Twenty-six per cent of tenants completed the survey, which asked if residents were experiencing problems with windows, doors, roofs, damp and heating. Eighty-five per cent of respondents said they were having problems with one or more of these. The most significant finding was that 61 per cent of respondents said damp was a problem in their home.

While a noticeable increase in remedial works did occur in the period after the publication of all four reports, the problems did not go away. Residents and local politicians continued to highlight the impact of defective building on the quality of their homes and its impact on their families' health and well-being.

In 2014 Balgaddy was included as one of twenty local authority estates that brought a collective complaint against the Irish state to the European Committee of Social Rights in Strasbourg, France. The complaint was coordinated by the Community Action Network and formally lodged by the International Federation for Human Rights. At the centre of the complaint was the charge that the councils' failure to maintain their housing stock to an adequate standard was a violation of the European Social Charter.[24]

Meanwhile, South Dublin County Council continued to claim that 'there is no systemic construction defect in Balgaddy causing dampness or structural issues, and that all identified defects have been remedied'.[25]

On 31 January 2018, the Committee of Ministers of the Council of Europe confirmed that in the case of the Federation of Human Rights Collective Complaint on behalf of residents of twenty local authority housing estates, the Irish state was in breach of Article 16 of the European Social Charter. That article vindicates the right of the family to social, legal and economic protection.

In their findings, the Committee of Ministers said they had seen 'evidence which demonstrates that a number of local authority tenants reside in poor housing conditions amounting to housing that is inadequate in nature'.[26] The Committee of Ministers concluded that 'The Government has failed to take sufficient and timely measures to ensure the right to housing of an adequate standard for not an insignificant number of families.'[27]

In May 2019, over a year after the Committee of Ministers' decision, widespread complaints about damp and defects were still being raised by residents in Balgaddy. Kitty Holland reported in *The Irish Times* that a Community Action Network survey of tenants' homes featured in the collective complaint confirmed that they were still having problems.[28] Holland reported tenants in Tor an Rí experiencing leaks and damp arising from structural defects.

In response, South Dublin County Council told Holland that they were committed to addressing 'legacy issues' and had, a month earlier, agreed an 'accelerated maintenance programme' to 'replace windows and doors, complete safety works and upgrade heating systems'.[29]

In response to a parliamentary question from the author on what action it had taken to address the article breach in Balgaddy, the Minister for Housing, Darragh O'Brien, told the Dáil on 14 January 2021 that 'Government have given careful consideration to the report'. He went on to say, 'my Department is committed to ensuring that tenants in social housing are provided with adequate housing that meets the standards most recently laid down in the Housing (Standards for Rented Housing) Regulations 2019'.

Two months later, in *The Irish Times*, Kitty Holland reported again from Balgaddy. She quoted Dr Padraic Kenna of the Centre for Housing Law at NUI Galway saying, 'there has been "no real change" in the "dire conditions" many Council tenants must endure'.[30] Holland quoted Balgaddy resident and healthcare worker Mary Cooney, who 'continues to live with black mould extending across her living-room and down the walls', and said, 'It's like Angela's Ashes in here sometimes.'

In April 2021 the European Committee on Social Rights released an updated report on a number of collective complaints involving the Irish state, including that related to Balgaddy. While they noted some progress from central and local government, they nonetheless concluded that the state continues to breach tenants' Article 16 rights.

An Ever-growing List

Priory Hall, Áras na Cluaine, Long Boat Quay, Millfield Manor, Foxford Court, Balgaddy, Belmayne, Galloping Green, Carrickmines Green and Brú na Sionna are just ten of an ever-growing list of Celtic Tiger-era housing developments in which building defects were not discovered by the self-certification regime put in place by the Fianna Fáil government in 1990. But the list is much longer than just these ten developments. In recent years, more and more owners have been forced to go public with their defects.

River Walk Court in Ratoath, County Meath, was built in 2002 by Michael Ryan's Saltan Properties. Defects, including an absence of fire stopping between the duplexes and apartments, and inadequate fire compartmentalisation in the communal areas, were discovered in 2011. Forty-two homes were affected, with an estimated cost of €1.5 million.[31]

Feltrim Hall in Holywell, Swords, County Dublin was built in 2002 by Albany Homes. Houses and apartments sold for up to €500,000 at the height of the Celtic Tiger. Fingal County Council discovered defects in its social housing units in the development in 2007, but private homeowners only became aware of the defects in 2012. A report by the council in that year discovered eleven different defects, including 'non-completion of fire stopping, openings cut in a wall to mount gas boilers, serious non-compliance in the location of gas risers and fire-resistant plasterboard not being carried to the full height of the walls'.[32]

The cost to the council to remediate their forty-four units was between €15,000 and €20,000.[33] The owners' management company has applied a levy of on average €12,000 on each owner to cover the cost of remediation of the most serious defects in their homes.

Spencer Dock, in Dublin 1, was built in 2004 by Treasury Holdings, owned by Johnny Ronan and Richard Barrett. The luxury apartments that once sold for up to €665,000 are now worth a fraction of that due to defects with balconies and windows causing damp and water ingress. As many as 150 homes are affected.[34]

Beacon South Quarter in Sandyford, south County Dublin, was built by Paddy Shovlin's Landmark Enterprises in 2005. Over 200 apartment owners and the approved housing body Clúid have been left with costs of between €10 million and €20 million to address fire-safety and water-ingress defects.[35]

Cathedral Court is a 104-unit apartment block in Clanbrassil Street, Dublin 8. Built in 2006 by Sherborough Enterprises Ltd, the company retained ownership of sixty-four of the apartments. Sherborough is run by the hotelier Noel O'Callaghan, and lists his three sons, Paul, Charles and Bryan, as directors. Their hotels include The Alex, The Green, The Davenport and The Mont in Dublin, as well as hotels in Gibraltar and Cambridge.[36]

When building defects were discovered in Cathedral Court in 2016, the owners' management company informed owners that they would be levied €5,000. Owners objected to the proposal as made by Paul O'Callaghan, who is one of the two directors on the OMC board. As Sherborough own sixty-four of the 105 apartments, they have a majority vote at any extraordinary general meeting at which decisions related to the cost of the remediation would be taken.[37]

Simonsridge is a 632-apartment development in Sandyford, County Dublin, built in 2006 by Shannon Homes, one of the state's oldest and most reputable home builders. Founded in the 1970s by the brothers Joseph and Sean Stanley, it has been run by Joseph's sons since his retirement in the 2000s. The founder and CEO of Cairn Homes, Michael Stanley, is Joseph's son and one of five brothers involved in Stanley Homes.

In 2019 owners in Simonsridge discovered significant defects, including an absence of fire stopping and fire-safety issues in the communal areas. The total cost of the works required to make the buildings comply with fire-safety standards is estimated to be €10 million.[38] Negotiations between Shannon Homes and the Simonsridge owners' management company led to an offer of a €1 million contribution from the developer to the cost of remediation. Owners voted to charge a levy of €2,000, which, along with the Shannon Homes monies, would allow works to commence.

However, as reported by Jack Horgan Jones and Niamh Towey in *The Irish Times* in 2020, the deal fell apart when Shannon Homes set a series of conditions on their financial contribution, including a requirement that '100 per cent of OMC members vote to accept an indemnity to Shannon Homes with respect to any future litigation from owners' and that 'apartment owners would also give an undertaking not to make a submission to An Bórd Pleanála regarding a nearby project currently being developed by Shannon Homes'.[39]

Throughout the course of 2019 and 2020, more and more defects cases were coming to light: Hyde Square in Kilmainham, Dublin 8, developed by Gerald and Mary Purcell Megard Ltd, with a remediation cost of €10,000 per affected apartment; Mansfield Avenue in Clongriffin, north Dublin, with a remediation cost of over €800,000; St James Wood, Kilmainham, Dublin 8, developed by Cosgrave Property Group, with a remediation cost of €1.78 million; Ath Lethan, Dundalk, County Louth, built by McGreevey enterprises, with a remediation cost of €1.4 million.

The Construction Defects Alliance, a campaign group made up of owners of properties with latent defects, is aware of a total of fifty-four residential developments comprising more than 10,000 homes with significant structural defects. All of these developments were built after the Building Control Act 1990 came into force. In none of these cases did the self-certification regime for building standards or fire-safety standards detect any defects.

A Partial Reform

In the immediate aftermath of the pyrite and Priory Hall defects scandals, the then Minister for the Environment, Fine Gael's Phil Hogan, established the High-Level Group on Building Control. The group was made up of two civil servants from the Department of the Environment, Community and Local Government, a representative from the Local Government Management Agency and the Chief Executive of the Housing Agency.

They were tasked to 'review the arrangements in place for building control activity and to make recommendations for its reform'.[40] Following a detailed consultation with industry, the group reported back to the minister and, in 2013, he announced his plans.

Foremost in Minister Hogan's mind was 'restoring consumer confidence in construction as an industry'.[41] The minister told the media, 'The new Building Control Regulations are a major step forward and will, for the first time, give home-owners, traceability and accountability at all stages of the building process.'[42] Hogan promised that his new regulations 'will provide consumers with the protection they need and deserve'.[43]

The minister's announcement referred to a package of measures that, taken together, aimed to strengthen the building control regime and prevent future Priory Halls. The proposed package was to include a new certification system, a new framework for building control authorities, a register of construction industry professionals and an examination of the issue of latent defects insurance.

Writing in *The Irish Times* in November 2013, Tony Reddy, Chairman of Reddy Architecture+Urbanism and former president of the Royal Irish Architectural Association, commented on the draft regulations then in circulation. His opinion piece detailed how 'much of the focus of departmental officials ... has been on the proposed new inspection and certification system for professionals and builders'.[44] He welcomed that 'Progress has also been made by the Construction Industry Federation' on a system of voluntary registration of builders to be introduced in 2014.'[45]

Nevertheless, he expressed some frustration that 'with just 14 weeks to go to the commencement of the new regulations, there is little evidence of significant progress on latent defects insurance or on specific oversight and inspection requirements for building control authorities'.[46] Reddy lamented the fact that 'This lack of momentum lies in an understandable, but misguided, policy of avoiding potential financial exposure for the State arising from failures of building control.'[47]

From the consumer's point of view, Reddy commented that even with the new system of professional inspection and certification, 'costly litigation may be necessary to resolve issues' where problems arise.[48] He also expressed concern that the language around local authority inspections was 'vague' and 'not enough to protect consumers'.[49] He urged Minister Hogan to 'direct his officials to amend the final draft of his code of practice so that Building Control Authorities must deliver a defined and measurable risk-based approach to inspection and compliance-checking'.[50]

The regulations, *Statutory Instrument Number 9 of 2014*, were published in January 2014. Known as the Building Control Amendment Regulations (BCAR), they did not actually change the existing building regulations. Rather, they introduced a new certification process whereby qualified professionals would have to inspect developments on behalf of the developer and submit certificates of compliance with the local authority. A certificate of completion would also have to be lodged with the local authority before a property could be legally occupied.

Councils still would not have an obligation to inspect the development. The assumption was that the certifier for say design, fire safety or disability access – now staking their professional reputation on the line by signing off on a cert – would be compelled to ensure the building was compliant with the regulations. An online Building Control Management System was to be established – managed by the City and County Managers Association – giving local authority building control staff access to the certifications of compliance in real time.

A guidance document for councils with a common protocol for the exercise of building control functions was to be adopted by the County and City Managers Association in July 2014. Meanwhile Construction Industry Register Ireland, located within the offices of the Construction Industry Federation, was established on a voluntary basis in 2014.

Kevin Hollingsworth, chairperson of the building surveying professional group of the Society of Chartered Surveyors Ireland, gave his view of the new building control regulations – now known as Statutory Instrument 9 (or S.I. 9) – in an opinion article in *The Irish Times* in February

2014, a month after the regulations were introduced.[51] While he welcomed the 'clear and auditable trail of responsibility for buildings' that S.I. 9 introduced, he had a number of significant concerns. 'The downside of this', he wrote, 'is that if anyone purchases a defective property under this new system, they will most likely have to take the costly route through the court to get redress.'[52]

Hollingsworth was also concerned with 'a potential conflict of interest in the new regime' where 'the assigned certifier can be an employee of the developer'.[53] He also urged government to give 'serious consideration' to the 'allocation of local authority resources for higher targeted inspection levels'.[54]

The combination of a more traceable certification regime, a register of construction professionals, an improved building control function within local authorities and the possibility of mandatory latent defects insurance, it was hoped, would strengthen the building control regime introduced in 1990 without fundamentally altering the system.

The success of Phil Hogan's reform would depend on all four elements progressing together and with equal force. Unfortunately, as has so often been the case when it comes to issues of building regulations and public safety, this was not how things panned out.

CHAPTER NINE

Inaction, Anger and Breakthrough

As more and more Celtic Tiger-era latent defects cases came to light, the issue of redress was placed firmly on the political agenda. So too was the broader issue of whether the state's building control regime – even after former minister Phil Hogan's 2014 reforms – was fit for purpose.

The review and reform of the building control system took place at a time when the supply of new homes had collapsed to levels not seen for decades. Revised figures published by the Central Statistics Office in 2020 showed that new home completions fell from 6,994 in 2011 to 4,575 in 2013.[1]

While the downward trend was reversed the following year, with an increase in output to 5,518, the new upward direction would be slow.

The result was an ever-growing gap between supply and demand across all sectors: social, private rental and owner occupation. As the economy moved out of recession from 2014, a new and ever-accelerating housing crisis would come to dominate the political agenda.

The February 2016 general election result made the formation of a new government unusually difficult. In took sixty-three days for an administration to be formed. Fianna Fáil facilitated the functioning of a minority Fine Gael administration through a confidence and supply agreement, abstaining on key votes including budgets and no confidence motions.

During the interregnum, the Dáil established a temporary subcommittee to examine the growing housing crisis. In June of that year the committee published its report, with over 100 recommendations for a change in housing policy. The new government – which for the first time included a dedicated Minister for Housing, Simon Coveney – published their new housing plan, *Rebuilding Ireland*, the following month.

While the issue of building control was not part of either the Dáil subcommittee report or the government plan, given the fact that both were calling for a major increase in the number of new homes to be delivered annually, building control and latent defects were inevitably going to find their way onto the agenda of the Housing Committee of the 32nd Dáil.

Safe as Houses?

In 2017, at the request of the author, the Joint Oireachtas Committee on Housing, Planning and Local Government agreed to include a review of the building control regime in their annual work programme for that year. Three dedicated public hearings took place on 5 and 13 April, with presentations from the Department of Housing, Planning and Local Government and representatives from the Irish

Planning Institute, the Society of Chartered Surveyors in Ireland and the Construction Industry Federation. Expert testimony was also provided by fire-safety professional Eamon O'Boyle, Professor of Architecture at University College Dublin Orla Hegarty, and Trinity College law PhD candidate and practising lawyer Deirdre Ní Fhloinn.

The committee also received written submissions from residents affected by latent defects in Beacon South Quarter, Millfield Manor and Longboat Quay, and from Engineers Ireland, the Royal Institute of Architects, the Institute of Civil Engineers, Marsh Ireland and architect Mel Reynolds.

In the first of the three hearings, the committee heard from Hubert Fitzpatrick of the Construction Industry Federation. He outlined the changes that had come into force since the introduction of S.I. 9 in 2014, and he argued that 'BCAR has introduced greater transparency, traceability and accountability across all companies in the construction industry'.[2] He also updated deputies on progress with the Construction Industry Register and reaffirmed his organisation's commitment to 'standards in the industry'.[3]

Deirdre Ní Fhloinn, a solicitor specialising in construction law for fourteen years, highlighted a number of shortcomings with the 2014 regulations. She said, 'Irish law is stacked against home-owners who discover defects.'[4] Of particular concern to Ní Fhloinn was the absence of transferable warranties and mandatory latent defects insurance. She questioned why government had never implemented the recommendation of the Law Reform Commission in their reports of 1977 and 1982 to place 'a statutory duty' on builders 'to ensure the work is undertaken in a good and workmanlike manner'.[5] Ní Fhloinn also argued strongly for the creation of a single 'building control authority' to oversee the building control system.

Eamon O'Boyle, a chartered engineer specialising in fire safety since 2002, talked the committee through the kinds of fire-safety defects that had emerged during the Celtic Tiger era and the weaknesses in the pre-2014 building control regime. He also contrasted the post-2014 certification system in Ireland with the system that was currently in place in Britain, saying that the Irish government had 'effectively outsourced [certification] to the private sector'.[6]

O'Boyle stressed that 'there are significant fire safety issues associated with some of the building stock nationally' and suggested, 'It is possible to address these issues in a proportionate way by undertaking a national programme of fire risk assessments.'[7]

After a detailed question and answer session, the committee adjourned. The following week, on 13 April, the committee resumed, hearing first from Orla Hegarty from the UCD School of Architecture. She too was critical of the weaknesses in the 2014 building control regulations. To address these, she recommended a number of legal and policy changes. She argued that the building control inspection regime should be independent of the developer and that there was a need for 'a national standard for substantial compliance, so everybody knows exactly what they are standing over'.[8] Hegarty also called for 'a strategy to look at construction industry insurance' and for 'market surveillance of construction products'. She stressed the need for 'a consumer support … through a portal for information which gives them clear advice' when dealing with the issue of defects.[9]

Alan Baldwin, a chartered building surveyor, spoke on behalf of the Society of Chartered Surveyors, which, he said, was 'supportive of the new building control regime', describing it as 'a significant improvement from what was in place previously'.[10] However, he was critical of the opt-out provision for one-off houses introduced by Alan Kelly when he was Minister for the Environment in 2015, saying that 'Government should ensure all builders are subject to the same standards set down in BCAR'.[11] Baldwin reiterated the society's position that there was a need for 'additional resourcing of independent oversight by local authority inspection staff to support a culture of transparency, traceability and accountability'.[12]

In his conclusion he also called for an examination of 'high-risk, multi-unit residential buildings, built in the recent past' to detect the scale of the latent defects issue, along with an 'emergency fund' to address 'the most urgent issues'.[13] The society also felt that placing the Construction Industry Register on a statutory footing was needed 'to protect consumers in the future against recurring defects'.[14]

After over an hour of further detailed questioning, the committee was suspended to allow representatives of the Department of Housing to take their positions for what would be the final of the three hearings.

Sarah Neary, principal advisor in the Built Environment Advisory Unit in the department, took members through the recent reforms of the building control system, including the introduction of the 2014 Building Control Amendment Regulations, the online Building Control Management System and the Construction Industry Register. She also informed the committee that the legislation to place the register on a statutory footing would be 'presented to Government for consideration shortly'.[15]

Shifting the focus away from what other contributors felt were weaknesses in the building control regime, Neary argued strongly that 'The failures of the past in construction arose largely due to inadequate design, poor workmanship, the use of improper products or a combination of these.' She said that 'significant reforms' introduced in recent years 'have brought a new order and discipline to bear on construction projects and have created a culture of compliance'.[16]

With the hearings complete, a draft report was prepared for the committee by the present author – the final amended version of which was approved unanimously by all deputies and senators in December 2017. *Safe as Houses? A Report on Building Standards, Building Controls and Consumer Protection* was published on 24 January 2018.

The report provided a short summary of the key points from the three days of public hearings and the written submissions received by committee. It recognised that 'the 2014 reforms represent significant progress towards a more robust building control regime'. Nonetheless, the members of the committee concluded that significant additional reform was required 'to further improve building standards and to increase confidence in both the construction sector and the regulatory framework and to strengthen the protection of the consumer'.[17]

The report's recommendations were presented under four headings. The first called for the creation of a Building Standards and Consumer Protection Agency, structured along the lines of the Food Safety Authority and Environmental Protection Agency. The body would work with building control authorities to ensure 'greater levels of consistency and compliance'.[18]

The committee recommended a significant transformation of the Building Control Amendment Regulations to make it a fully independent inspection and certification process, led by local authorities. Protecting future home buyers from latent defects was the third area of proposed reforms, with a focus on mandatory latent defects insurance and a range of legal reforms long advocated by the Law Reform Commission.

Finally, the committee called for the establishment of a latent defects redress scheme and fund based on the principle that 'ordinary owners who purchased in good faith should not be liable for the costs of remediation caused by the incompetence, negligence or deliberate non-compliance of others'.[19] The report set out a number of options for the structure and financing of such a redress scheme, including a levy on the construction industry to be matched by exchequer funding.[20]

Writing in *The Irish Times* on the day of the report's launch, the present author said, 'We know the human and financial cost of failures like Priory Hall. The question is whether we have the political will to ensure our building control and consumer protection systems are robust enough to ensure such failures never happen again.'[21]

Safe as Houses? received mixed reviews. Homeowners of properties with latent defects and some industry professionals and academic experts welcomed it. Others, however, were more critical. In a detailed response on behalf of Dublin City Council, Senior Building Control Officer Pat Nestor criticised the failure of the committee to hear directly from building control authorities.[22] Nestor said that the 'overall tone of the Report is quite partisan in criticising the procedures introduced by BC(A)R in 2014' and that 'little documentary evidence is referenced in the report'.[23]

The letter was more positive on the report's recommendations regarding consumer protection and redress, saying they were 'very welcome particularly dealing with the potential for latent defects'.[24] With respect to the proposal for a latent defects redress scheme, Nestor wrote, 'While there is a logic in this recommendation the onus should be on the construction sector to provide such a scheme.'[25]

A short Dáil debate on *Safe as Houses?* was held on 24 May 2018. Committee members, including chairperson and Fine Gael TD Maria Bailey and the present author, outlined the key findings of the report. In response, Minister for Housing Eoghan Murphy rejected the depiction of the 2014 Building Regulations as self-certification, because 'For the majority of projects, design and assigned certifiers are independent of the builder.'

The minister also reiterated the government's long-standing position that 'building defects are matters for resolution between the contracting parties involved: the homeowner, the builder, the developer and/or their respective insurers, structural guarantee or warranty scheme'.

Significantly, the recently appointed Fianna Fáil housing spokesperson, Darragh O'Brien, who had not participated in the hearings or the drafting of the report, spoke in favour of its recommendations. He described the building control regime 'as it is now' as 'not fit for purpose and could be improved greatly'.[26]

Private Members' Motion

The real value of the *Safe as Houses?* report was that it pushed the issue of building control and latent defects up the political and media agenda. In doing so it gave voice to a wider range of interested parties than just the construction industry. It also gave a platform to homeowners struggling to understand the complex legal and regulatory environment in which they now found themselves.

While the *Safe as Houses?* report was being drafted, Green Party TD Catherine Martin tabled a Dáil Private Members' Motion on Building Standards, Regulations and Homeowner Protection in June 2017. The motion acknowledged that thousands of homeowners were affected by 'poor quality homes' and that the 'record of the current Government and the Previous Government is one of clear failure to properly regulate the building industry'.[27] The motion was critical of the 2014 Building Control Amendment Regulations for failing to address these problems and supportive of the recommendations on defective buildings in the Law Reform Commission's 1977 and 1982 reports. It also made a series of proposals for further government action, including legislating for transmissible warranties, reviewing existing building contracts, establishing a state-wide building authority, amending the statute of limitations, and putting in place a consumer-friendly dispute resolution process for dealing with defects and a fund to cover the costs of remediation.

Proposing the motion, Catherine Martin TD, who had been working with residents from Beacon South Quarter in her own constituency of Dublin Rathdown, said:

> The motion calls on the Government to properly tackle the sorry legacy of defects in housing construction and to strengthen building standards and regulations in order to safeguard against this

building and regulatory failure ever recurring. This and the previous Government have shown no political appetite or given no priority to dealing effectively with serious problems and issues arising from appalling construction quality of so many homes built during the boom-time era.[28]

Concluding her opening remarks, Deputy Martin referred to the tragic Grenfell Tower fire, which only days earlier had claimed the lives of seventy-two people, injuring seventy more. She urged TDs to put safety at the forefront of their minds when considering the issues at hand. She said:

> The tragic inferno in west London last week is a stark reminder that the overriding priority underpinning all construction must be the safety of residents. In the rush to build the houses so urgently needed in this country, we must ensure that this time we do it right and that all houses are built to an acceptable and safe standard. The Members of this House have a duty to create a legislative framework to support all those who are living the nightmare of having had defects discovered in their homes and to prevent this happening to another generation of home owners.[29]

The motion was broadly supported by the opposition. Though Fianna Fáil unsuccessfully tabled a detailed amendment, they supported the Green Party motion, ensuring its successful passage when the vote was formally taken on 22 June.

Speaking during the debate, their Housing Committee member Pat Casey welcomed the motion and detailed the ongoing work of the committee on the *Safe as Houses?* report, stressing that 'We have to move from the current system of what is still self-certification and move to a robust, independent and rigorous inspection system that is controlled by the State.'[30]

A Sinn Féin amendment drafted in the wake of the Grenfell tragedy was tabled by the present author, who spoke during the debate, outlining Sinn Féin's support for the Green Party motion. The amendment, which was supported by Deputy Martin, called on the government to 'conduct an urgent review of the use of combustible materials used in the construction and refurbishment of homes and to update, if necessary, fire safety regulations; and conduct an urgent review of fire safety compliance and enforcement regulations and bring forward new regulations, if necessary, to ensure the highest safety standards in residential dwellings'.

For their part, the government tabled their own countermotion, sharing some of the sentiment of the Green Party text but opposing Deputy Martin's reform proposals and supporting what they believed was the success of the 2014 Building Control Amendment Regulations. In a wide-ranging speech, Minister for Housing Eoghan Murphy, outlining the government's position and using a formula of words that was to become the standard response from Fine Gael when responding to calls for a latent defects redress scheme, said:

> In general, building defects are matters for resolution between the contracting parties involved: the homeowner, the builder, the developer and-or their respective insurers, structural guarantee or warranty scheme. In this regard, it is incumbent on the parties

responsible for poor workmanship and-or the supply of defective materials to accept their responsibilities and take appropriate action to provide remedies for affected homeowners. It is not possible for the State to take on responsibility or liability for all legacy issues of defective building materials or workmanship. More than that though, it would not send the right message to the industry regarding their responsibility for compliance and it might lead to unnecessary risk taking given the financial liability for any failures would be borne by the taxpayer. Why remove this responsibility from builders and put it on taxpayers when builders have a responsibility and a liability which can be effectively policed and controlled?[31]

Nobody on the opposition benches during the debate proposed that builders or developers should be absolved of shouldering the responsibility for fixing defective buildings. But the suggestion that defects, particularly pre-2014 defects, were purely a private matter between builders and home buyers, was to ignore the difficulties homeowners had in securing such redress, particularly when the developer had gone into liquidation. It also ignored the very real failure of government to put in place an adequate regulatory regime that protected buyers and provided them access to redress when defects were discovered.

The passing of the motion was a significant, if purely symbolic, victory for the growing number of homeowners and tenants living in defective buildings. While it failed to force the government into any meaningful action on the issue, it further highlighted the plight of owners of defective properties.

The Construction Defects Alliance

Throughout 2018 and 2019, media interest in Celtic Tiger latent defects increased. As more and more owners came forward to tell their story, opposition TDs and senators continued to press the government for both a latent defects redress scheme and further reform of the building control system.

Fine Gael's inaction on the issue first generated anger. But in turn, owners started to network and organise, leading to the formation of the Construction Defects Alliance in the autumn of 2019. The alliance emerged out of efforts of owners in Beacon South Quarter to address the significant defects in that development. Clúid, the approved housing body, with units in the development, offered to assist in providing organisational support.

The alliance described themselves as 'an informal grouping focused on getting redress for apartment owners as proposed by the Oireachtas Housing Committee'.[32] Specifically they were campaigning for the implementation of the *Safe as Houses?* report, including 'The establishment of a redress scheme to assist homeowners with latent defects; Provision of an information and advice service for those affected by defects; Redress scheme to be funded through industry levy matched by Government funding, tax write offs or interest-free loans.'[33]

On Thursday, 7 November 2019, the Construction Defects Alliance was invited to present their case to the Joint Oireachtas Committee on Housing, Planning and Local Government, almost two years on from the completion of the *Safe as Houses?* report.[34] Committee members heard from Kath Cottier of Clúid, Des McCabe of the Apartment

Owners Network and Matt Cleary and Andrew Prior, both owners of defective apartments.

During the meeting Cottier estimated that as many as 92,000 apartments could be affected by Celtic Tiger defects.[35] The figure was based on an assessment by Keenan Property Management of their own apartment stock, which revealed that up to 70 per cent had building defects of some kind.[36]

She talked the committee through the experience of owners who discovered defects in their homes and the emotional and financial impact it was having on them. She also made the case for a redress scheme and, while calling for the full implementation of the *Safe as Houses?* recommendations, she urged government to consider some interim measures, such as 'soft loans to ease the pain of owners who are having to pay levies' to remediate their properties.[37]

During the debate, the new Fianna Fáil housing spokesperson, Darragh O'Brien, offered his support to the alliance. Reflecting on his experience of owners with pyrite in his constituency, he suggested that 'There is a roadmap as to how we can deal with this matter.'[38] He also supported the use of Home Building Finance Ireland, the government's new lending facility for builders, as a source of finance for owners' management companies. While supporting 'tax reliefs in the absence of a full remediation scheme', the Dublin North TD stressed that 'at the end of the day it is those who are responsible who should pay'.[39] O'Brien called for consideration to be given to 'retrospective' support for those who have already paid for remediation.

Within a matter of weeks, the Taoiseach, Leo Varadkar, dissolved the Dáil when it became clear that Fianna Fáil would not abstain on a no-confidence motion in the Minister for Health to be tabled by Sinn Féin. A general election was called for February 2020.

Breakthrough

The Construction Defects Alliance seized on the opportunity presented to them by the election. They organised an email lobby urging TDs and their parties to commit to a redress scheme in their manifestos. Thousands of people affected by defects – many in developments that were not yet in the public domain – emailed prospective Dáil deputies, insisting that the incoming government must address the Celtic Tiger defects issue.

Over two years of campaigning – by owners, supportive politicians and others – was to prove successful. All parties bar Fine Gael committed to some form of latent defects redress in the 2020 general election.

The Fianna Fáil manifesto promised to continue funding the pyrite and mica remediation scheme. Importantly they pledged to

> Put in place loan funding to help address apartment defects. The remit of Home Building Finance Ireland should be expanded to encompass loan finance to Owner Management Companies who are undertaking remedial work on defective buildings. These owners who purchased in good faith deserve additional support. Furthermore, rogue builders should have no place in our construction sector. We will:
>
> Revise the remit of HBFI to expand funding to Owner Management Companies including clarity

around access and conditions. Place a bar on the awarding of publicly-funded construction project tenders should be [sic] introduced to prevent such contracts from being awarded to developers/builders or associated construction professionals found to be in serious breach of building standards or fire safety regulation. Put in place a €10m latent defect scheme as an initial allocation to address legacy issues in certain developments.[40]

Sinn Féin had included a costed and comprehensive latent defects redress scheme in their Alternative Budget for 2021, with an initial fund of €15 million and contributions from industry and government. In their election manifesto they reaffirmed their commitment to the issue. The document said that in government, Sinn Féin would

Fully implement the 2017 Joint Oireachtas Committee on Housing, Planning and Local Government report Safe as Houses? including the creation of a Building Control Agency, a reformed BCAR process and a latent defects redress scheme for owners of Celtic Tiger properties with latent defects.[41]

The Green Party also committed to 'Implementing the recommendations of the "Safe as Houses?" report', as well as 'Enacting our Homeowner Protection Bill to ensure that builders and developers have a duty to purchasers of residential property and to subsequent owners to build the dwelling properly.' They pledged to establish 'an independent building standards regulator, exempting defective homes from property taxes, and establishing a scheme of financial assistance, such as low-cost loan finance and tax relief, to assist with the cost of repairing defects'.[42]

As the election campaign was coming to a close, initial predictions of a significant Fianna Fáil advance did not materialise. A Sinn Féin surge in the final weeks caught everybody by surprise. The results were equally as dramatic, with both Fianna Fáil and Fine Gael losing votes and seats, and Sinn Féin, the Green Party and the Social Democrats all gaining.

In what was described by many as a 'change election', Sinn Féin emerged as the largest party in terms of votes, but failure to stand more candidates left Mary Lou McDonald's party trailing Fianna Fáil by a single seat in the Dáil chamber. When veteran Fianna Fáil TD Seán Ó Fearghaíl was re-elected as Ceann Comhairle on 20 February, Sinn Féin and Fianna Fáil were on even numbers.

For four months, parties tried to form a government – a job made difficult by the fact that no two parties could form a majority. The imposition of Covid-19 restrictions from mid-March added to the protracted nature of the negotiations, with the Green Party formally withdrawing from talks with all parties for a period while calling for a government of national unity to deal with the pandemic. Eventually, Micheál Martin was elected Taoiseach on 27 June, leading a historic coalition government made up of Fianna Fáil, Fine Gael and a deeply divided Green Party.

The 125-page programme for government was titled 'Our Shared Future'. It was the longest programme in the history of the state. Page 56 included a subheading of 'Defects', which read:

We will:

Examine the issue of defective housing in the first 12 months, having regard to the recommendations of the Joint Oireachtas Committee on Housing report, 'Safe as Houses'.

Bring forward law reform to improve the legal remedies for homeowners who are dealing with defects.

Ensure that the remediation fund for Pyrite and Mica is fully drawn down.

Assist owners of latent defect properties, by identifying options for those impacted by defects, to access low-cost, long-term finance.[43]

Like much of the programme for government, the commitments were heavily caveated with language like 'examine', 'having regard for', 'assist' and 'identify options'. Significantly the only financing option referenced in the programme was low-cost finance rather than an industry levy or exchequer funding. But, importantly, for the first time since the scandal of latent defects was first brought to light, a government was engaging with the issue beyond just pyrite and mica. For owners of Celtic Tiger defects homes and their supporters, this was an important step forward.

Taoiseach Micheál Martin appointed Dublin North TD Darragh O'Brien as the new Minister for Housing, Local Government and Heritage. In September O'Brien announced his intention to establish a working group to examine the issue of building defects and funding options including low-cost loans and tax breaks.

Addressing the Joint Oireachtas Committee on Housing, Heritage and Local Government in December 2020, Kath Cottier of the Construction Defects Alliance told members that 'The commitments in the programme for Government to examine the issue of defective housing in the first 12 months having regard to the recommendations of the 'Safe as Houses' report is the first serious effort by Government to address the matter of legacy defects, and that is why the alliance warmly welcomes it.'[44]

However, Cottier also made clear the Alliance's view on who should pay for remediating the defects, saying:

> It is important that committee members and the Government are absolutely clear on our position. Access to cheap loans on their own, whether with no interest or very low interest, would not be acceptable to the Construction Defects Alliance as a solution for tackling the costs of remediation. While they would ease the cash flow pressure on OMCs and owners, they would still leave the owners 100% on the hook for remediating defects they did not in any way cause. The very least the alliance would accept would be a combination of soft loans and tax breaks or a financial equivalent.[45]

She stressed the importance of ensuring that financial supports would be 'retrospective' for those who have already paid for their properties to be made safe.

While the process put in train by Minister O'Brien was modelled on that used by his predecessor Phil Hogan in addressing the pyrite scandal, there was one important difference. The minister had given a guarantee that both the

Construction Defects Alliance and the Apartment Owners Network would be represented on the working group. He said the group would be asked to report back to him by June 2020 and that its findings would assist in formulating the government's response in advance of Budget 2022.

Minister O'Brien appointed former Donegal County Council chief executive Séamus Neely to chair the working group, which met for the first time on 26 March 2021. Both the Construction Defects Alliance and the Apartment Owners Network were represented on the group alongside representatives of the architecture, chartered surveyor and fire-safety professions, and officials from the Departments of Finance and Housing.

At the time of writing, the working group's report deadline of June 2021 will not be met. Nevertheless, if the group is to have any impact on Budget 2022, it will have to formulate recommendations for government in advance of October 2021, when the budget is announced.

The experience of the pyrite panel shows that there can also be a delay between the publication of a report and government action. It took Phil Hogan two years to draft and pass the legislation for the pyrite remediation scheme.

Owners of houses and apartments with Celtic Tiger defects don't have two years to wait. Many are currently facing significant levies for remediation of their homes, which, if not paid, will result in loss of insurance cover or legal action from the owners' management company. Others are trapped in potentially unsafe apartments, unsure of the extent of the danger, with no prospect of remediation in the short to medium term, as their management company is locked in legal proceedings with receivers or developers.

And there are those, like Ciara Holland in Galloping Green, for whom it is a matter of principle. She told the Oireachtas committee in December 2020, 'I have done everything and anything I can to try to get justice and I vow that I will keep working on this until I do and my developer is held accountable for what he has done to us.'[46]

There is an expectation from homeowners that Minister O'Brien will keep his word and act with the urgency that the issue deserves.

CHAPTER TEN

The Case for Real Reform

Phil Hogan's 2014 reforms of the building control system did not fundamentally alter the regime that had been put in place by the Building Control Act of 1990. While it improved the traceability of the certification process, it failed to provide a fully independent inspection regime or an adequate mechanism of redress for owners who, through no fault of their own, had bought defective homes.

Significantly it was silent on the issue of Celtic Tiger latent defects. The government position – that defects are a private matter between the builder/developer and the purchaser – completely ignores the fact that bad building is more likely to happen in a weak regulatory environment. The weaker that regulatory framework, the greater the level of non-compliance.

Of course, the primary responsibility for defects lies with the developer and builder (who are sometimes one and the same). But that does not absolve the state for its own failing to ensure that the building control regime, put in place to ensure buildings are constructed in accordance with clear standards, was robust and provided the public with the greatest level of protection.

Repeatedly, governments refused to listen to advice from opposition politicians and professionals in the construction industry, who called for an independent inspection regime and stronger consumer protections. Indeed, the government not only effectively allowed the industry to police itself through self-certification but also systematically underfunded local authorities and their building control departments, leaving them ill-equipped to deal with the volume of building – and, in turn, bad building – that took place during the Celtic Tiger property boom.

As we face into another significant increase in construction activity, there is an urgent need for more thoroughgoing reform of our building control system. This will require change in legislation and policy. It will also require a significant increase in the resourcing of those agencies tasked with ensuring our buildings are safe.

It is a telling feature of the history of building control in the state that it takes a tragedy often involving loss of life for reform to advance, whether the deaths in tenements in 1913 and 1963, the deaths in the Stardust nightclub in 1981 or the death of Fiachra Daly in 2013.

There is also a need to put in place a comprehensive latent defects redress scheme to ensure that all those affected by serious Celtic Tiger defects, including fire-safety issues, are supported in making their homes safe.

The proposals set out below, based in large part on the recommendations of the all-party Oireachtas Housing Committee report *Safe as Houses?*, are the present author's attempt to map out what that reform should look like.

Latent Defects Redress Scheme

The government should establish, as a matter of urgency,

a redress scheme to assist homeowners with latent defects. The mission statement of the scheme should be, 'Ordinary owners who purchased in good faith should not be liable for the costs of remediation caused by the incompetence, negligence or deliberate non-compliance of others.'

At the centre of the redress scheme should be a Latent Defects Redress Board with a number of specific functions, including the provision of information, mediation and legally binding adjudication. The function of the board should be to provide a non-judicial process for owners getting redress to remediate their homes.

A good model for the board would be the Residential Tenancies Board, which provides similar services for landlords and tenants in dispute. In the case of latent defects, the overriding approach should be to ensure that, in the first instance, the developer or builder responsible for the defects should pay the cost of remediation.

A free and independent information service to owners who discover defects should be provided to assist them in navigating the complex legal and financial issues involved. A mediation service to seek agreement between developers/builders and owners should also be available.

Importantly the board must have the power to impose legally binding adjudications where mediation is not possible or where it does not secure an agreement between the parties.

There will also be a need for a redress fund to cover the cost of remediation where the developer or builder is no longer solvent or trading. This fund should be made up of contributions from industry, through a levy, and from the exchequer. The amount of funding and the ratio of industry to government funding would be determined by the extent of the problem. While the total cost of remediating Celtic

Tiger defects is not yet known, it is likely that a multi-million annual budget will be required.

Government should seek the advice of the Attorney General to see whether the state can impose adjudication decisions on directors of companies where those directors have liquidated the company responsible for the defects while establishing a new company to continue operating in the construction sector.

Government should also adopt a policy whereby companies or directors of companies responsible for latent defects are not provided with any grant aid (such as the Local Infrastructure Housing Activation Fund) or public construction contracts where they are not cooperating with the Latent Defects Redress Board.

Similarly, amendments to planning law should be introduced to take into account the applicant's previous involvement in latent defects cases and the remediation of such when granting new permissions for new developments. It would also be useful to amend the planning acts to make compliance with building regulations a condition of planning. In turn, non-compliance, use of defective materials or poor workmanship resulting in defects could be subject to planning enforcement.

Initially the board would be demand-led, dealing with cases brought to its attention by owners. However, there is also a need for a proactive assessment of the extent of the problem. The board should have the capacity to instigate inspections at the request of owners, initially focusing on high-risk buildings – determined by type or by developer – built during those years in which known latent defects were most common.

The redress scheme must also provide some form of retrospective relief for those owners who have already covered the costs of remediating their homes. This could be done by way of allowing these homeowners to write off the capital costs of remediation against their future tax liabilities over a number of years, as is currently the case for landlords.

Building Standards Agency

As part of the post-2014 building control reforms, government created a National Building Control Office (NBCO), to provide 'oversight, direction and support for the development, standardisation and implementation of building control in local authorities'. The NBCO, based in Dublin, was allocated seven staff and was headed by former senior executive engineer in Fingal County Council Mairéad Phelan. A further seven staff have been allocated in 2020 for inspection of building materials entering Ireland from the UK as part of the Brexit withdrawal agreement process.

Nonetheless, given the scale and complexity of building control issues, there is a compelling argument for the NBCO to be expanded much further, into a fully-fledged independent Building Standards Agency. The model for such an agency would be the Food Standards Authority or the Environmental Protection Agency. Bodies with significant powers, staff and resources.

Importantly this new agency would not take over the functions of building control authorities in local authorities, who would still be responsible for inspections and enforcement. Nevertheless, the new agency would assist both the local authorities and government in ensuring that our building control regime was the most robust possible. It would continue and expand the current role of the NBCO in ensuring greater levels of consistency of compliance by local authorities as well as promoting best practice. It would also be the location for a number of building control-related functions, including the Latent Defects Redress Board and redress scheme, the Building Control Management System and the statutory Construction Industry Register and complaints process.

The agency would assist government and industry with policy development, research and data collection in a similar way to the supports currently provided to government by the Environmental Protection Agency, the Residential Tenancies Board and the Housing Agency. It could also have a role as a construction qualifications registration authority and work with industry, government and the education sector in developing world-class apprenticeships and lifelong trade skills development programmes.

In essence, the Building Standards Agency would become a state-wide hub for expertise in building control and provide a range of supports and functions for local authorities, government and industry to become a world leader in promoting high-quality, well-built, safe and zero-carbon buildings.

Making BCAR Truly Independent

While an improvement on the Building Control Act of 1990, the 2014 Building Control Amendment Regulations did not end the practice of self-certification. They simply made it more transparent. But it remains a form of self-certification whereby developers employ certifiers to sign off on building control compliance. The potential for conflicts of interest in this system is clear, and the risk of inappropriate certification is no less than was the case with the pre-2014 regime, particularly in any future construction boom.

In the view of the present author, the case for a fully independent inspection regime is compelling.

In order to completely break the self-certification element that remains with BCAR, design certifiers and assigned certifiers should be employed directly by local authorities, either on a contract basis or as full-time local authority employees. The costs of certification would remain with the developer/builder, who would pay local authorities directly in respect of fees, with no additional handling fee being levied by the local authority.

Neither design certifiers nor assigned certifiers should be employed by a developer/builder on either the project they are certifying or any other project with that developer in any other role. Clear terms of engagement and training will be required to assist the transition from developer-employed certifiers to local authority-appointed certification.

To ensure independent inspection on construction by local authorities, councils would not be allowed to self-certify or employ assigned certifiers for their own developments, such as social housing or other public facilities. This would be contracted out via the Building Standards Agency.

Resourcing of building control authorities would need to be increased to ensure they have the capacity to manage an ever-growing inspection and certification requirement, particularly in large urban areas.

There should also be mandatory fire-safety inspections by specialist building control officers on all units in multiple occupancy developments and developments with a higher level of fire risk before completion certificates are issued.

Protecting against Future Defects

The purpose of a robust and independent building control regime is to create an environment where compliance is high and the likelihood of bad building is greatly reduced. There will still be a need for further protections for home buyers against the possibility of future defects. Many of the measures detailed below have been recommended by the Law Reform Commission and other bodies for many years.

Latent defects insurance should be a legal requirement to be provided by the developer/builder on the sale of all new residential properties. While such defects insurance is becoming more widespread in the residential sector, there is simply no coherent argument against it being mandatory. Industry claims that it will increase the cost of development. However, given the very significant costs incurred, both by the state and homeowners, arising from Celtic Tiger defects, the small additional cost arising from mandatory defects insurance would be a welcome guarantee for most home buyers, who would know that should defects occur in the future, they will be fully protected.

There is also a need for transmissible warranties of quality from developers/builders and those involved in the building process in favour of the first and subsequent purchasers. This will require primary legislation and should be progressed by government as a matter of urgency.

A new statute of limitations that starts from discovery of defect rather than from purchase of the property should be introduced in the same legislation, as many structural defects are neither visible nor present at the point of purchase.

There is also a need for reform of the contracts used on home purchasing. Minimum mandatory terms for such contracts should be introduced to ensure a fair balance between the rights of the developer/builder and those of the purchaser.

A review of the existing sanctions and punishments for developers/builders who breach building and fire-safety standards should be undertaken, and appropriate reforms should be introduced via primary legislation to ensure a greater level of deterrent is in place for those tempted to break the law. There should also be a legal bar on the awarding of publicly funded construction project tenders to developers/builders or associated construction professionals found to be in serious breach of building standards or fire-safety regulations.

Conclusion

Phil Hogan's building control 2014 reforms were presented as a package: a new certification regime; a statutory register of construction industry professionals, including an independent complaints mechanism; an increased support for building control authorities, allowing for greater consistency across the authorities; and an examination of the issue of latent defects insurance to see how consumer protection could be enhanced.

Seven years on and only one element of this package has been fully implemented: the BCAR certification process. The Construction Industry Register has not been placed on a statutory footing, and no formal binding complaints process is available to home buyers. There has been no movement on the issue of making latent defects insurance more widely available, let alone mandatory, leaving homeowners with defects at the mercy of an expensive and lengthy legal route when seeking redress. And despite the very good work of the National Building Control Office, it is – as has always been the case with building control – understaffed, under-resourced and without any real power.

The consequence is that our building control system, while better than before, is nowhere near as robust as it should be. Consumers still do not have the level of protection that they deserve. Crucially the system is still open to abuse by rogue developers and builders.

While the relatively modest level of construction activity in recent years has not revealed widespread abuses of the building control regulations, are we really sure that in any future building boom, the kinds of problems that occurred during the Celtic Tiger would not occur again?

Can we say that the system is as robust as it could be? Can we say this with certainty to Ciara Holland, Mark, Lorraine and Gary Carew, Alan and Aine, Stephanie Meehan and her family and the thousands of other homeowners and tenants who, through no fault of their own, have been left living in defective and unsafe buildings?

Only through further legislative and policy reform, adequate resourcing of building control authorities and an increased focus on consumer protection through independent inspections can we ensure that our building control system is fit for purpose and that the state is providing people with the greatest degree of protection possible against defective buildings.

The Architect, the Supplier and the Building Control Officer ... and the West Awakes

Throughout the course of 2019 I had become aware of several instances where building regulations were not being adhered to. When I engaged – as I do regularly – with architects, building control officers, building suppliers and residents, serious breaches of both the building regulations and the BCAR certification process were being alleged by credible sources.

In December 2019 I wrote to the then Minister for Housing, Eoghan Murphy, outlining these cases. The email was cc'd to the secretary general of the department, senior departmental officials dealing with building control issues, and the National Building Control Office. I made clear in my email that I had no evidence to suggest that these types of breaches were widespread. Nevertheless, given that they were of a serious nature, and were allegedly occurring across the state, I felt it important that the minister and senior civil servants be made aware of them.

The Architect

While dealing with an unrelated planning matter, I came into contact with an architect who leads a mid-sized practice in Dublin. The company had a good reputation for designing and certifying small and mid-sized residential developments.

During the course of a wider conversation on what was happening in the industry, the architect told me of three separate developments on which he worked where three separate developers were not complying with either his architectural plans or the building regulations.

The architect was unwilling to certify non-compliant work and made that clear to the developers in each case. Significant pressure was applied by the developers, including threats of withholding payment for works completed to date.

In the end, unwilling to break the law, the architect walked off each of the three jobs – unpaid for a significant portion of the work his company had undertaken. In all three cases, a new certifier was appointed, the development proceeded, and the homes are now occupied.

When I asked the architect whether, in his opinion, such practice was widespread, he said that while he wouldn't use that word, he did feel that it was common.

The Supplier

In a separate engagement I was contacted, initially anonymously, by an individual who worked for a building supplier who specialised in fire-safety and insulation products. The individual was concerned with what he was seeing in a wide range of private and public sector building sites around the country.

A meeting with the individual was arranged, to which he brought a folder of photographs. He claimed that the images provided evidence of poor-quality work. The photographs clearly showed poor installation of insulation, fire-resistant barriers, fire stopping and other necessary works to protect against smoke and fire spread and to ensure legally required energy efficiency.

The supplier made clear that where he came across such issues, he raised them with the relevant foreman on site and outlined how the works should be remedied. However, he was unable to confirm whether the problems were rectified or left as in the photographs.

The supplier expressed a strong view that there were three problems leading to the defective works: a lack of clarity in the Department of Housing technical guidelines for insulation and fire safety; a lack of adequate training amongst some construction workers; and a lack of proper oversight on the site.

The supplier admitted that he did not know if these problems were identified at certification stage by the assigned certifier and in turn remedied. Nevertheless, it was the prevalence of the defective work that led him to approach me in the first instance.

The Building Control Officer

Building control is often seen as the poor relation to planning in local authority departments, where both functions are usually co-located. This can, at times, lead to conflicts where the planning authority may grant permission for a commercial or residential development that does not or cannot fully comply with building regulations.

During 2019 I was contacted, in confidence, by a building control officer in a mid-sized local authority. The individual was concerned that regular conflicts of interest were occurring between the planning and building control sections of the council. The consequence of these conflicts, the individual alleged, was resulting in regular breaches of building regulations and the completion of buildings with significant defects.

The officer had attempted to have these issues addressed within the chain of command in the local authority in question. However, as some of the conflicts related to granted planning permissions that, again in the words of the officer, could not comply with building regulations – in terms of materials being used and structural configurations of the buildings in question – the inevitable hierarchy that exists between senior planners and building control officers made it impossible to have the matter adequately addressed.

The officer was concerned that, in years to come, a number of commercial and residential developments would discover defects that could have been avoided if the advice of the building control section had been taken.

Fear of Going Public

TDs are often contacted by people who have come across what they believe is wrongdoing that they want exposed. Sometimes these people have an axe to grind or an ulterior motive. In other cases, they are genuine people who are seeing something wrong and want assistance in bringing it to light.

In the case of the architect, the supplier and the building control officer, my strong view is that they were all genuine cases of people who were trying to do the right thing. They came across something that was not compliant with building regulations and did not want to be part of it.

But these people have families; they have mortgages and bills to pay. The consequences of going public or raising the matter beyond a certain level brings with it the possibility of life-altering consequences, such as loss of employment.

In each case I asked if they would provide me with detailed information that I could bring to the attention of the minister, the Oireachtas Housing Committee or the media. But in all three cases the individuals concerned were too fearful of the consequences for their own livelihoods to take that risk. Given how whistle-blowers are often treated in this country, that reluctance is completely understandable.

The only route left to me as a TD was to bring the matters to the attention of the minister and his officials, albeit in the anonymised fashion that it had been presented to me. Despite the seriousness of the issues contained in my email to Minister Murphy, I never received a reply.

Larkfield House

Unlike the cases detailed above, the most serious breach of the 2014 Building Control Amendment Regulations to date is widely known to the public, the media, the relevant local authority and the Minister for Housing and his department.

Larkfield House, on the Coldcut Road in Clondalkin, Dublin 22, was formerly a gym run by Ben Dunne. It was subsequently sold to the developer Vincent Cosgrave, whose company, Cavvies, applied to convert the building into apartments.

A planning application was submitted to South Dublin County Council in July 2016 for thirty-seven apartments. The application was successful. However, rather than proceed with the development, Cosgrave submitted a second application in May 2017 to increase the number of apartments to forty-eight. This was refused.

Cavvies appealed the decision to An Bórd Pleanála. However, rather than waiting for the board to decide on the application, Cosgrave went ahead and converted the former gym into forty-eight apartments, and by early 2018 it was fully tenanted.

A significant number of the tenants were transferred from homeless emergency accommodation in Dublin City and placed in the development by the Dublin Regional Homeless Executive. The families, who finally hoped that they had secured long-term homes, were funded through the Homeless HAP (Housing Assistance Payment), which provided the landlord with a rent of up to €1,800 per month.

Before An Bórd Pleanála made their decision, South Dublin County Council became aware that the building had been refurbished and tenanted without either planning permission or the various certifications – including fire-safety and completion certificates – that were a legal requirement under the 2014 Building Control Amendment Regulations.

Eleven families residing in Larkfield House, who were South Dublin County Council social housing applicants, had their HAP applications refused because, in the view of that council, the building was not compliant with planning or building regulations.

In May 2018 An Bord Pleanála refused Cavvies' appeal, creating an immediate crisis for the company and, more importantly, the forty-plus households living in the building.

South Dublin County Council faced an appalling dilemma. How could they ensure the building was planning and building control compliant while at the same time avoiding making these families – many of whom had come from homelessness – homeless?

As a TD for the constituency in which Larkfield House is located, I began working with residents to assist them in avoiding homelessness. I engaged with the council's housing and planning departments, met with the developer and raised the matter informally with the Minister for Housing, Eoghan Murphy, and his departmental officials. While a fire-safety inspection deemed the building safe, there was an urgent need for the status of the building to be regularised.

In autumn 2018 Cosgrave applied for planning retention, with a proposal to reduce the development to thirty-seven units. South Dublin County Council approved the application that November, but under strict conditions. A full schedule of works had to be submitted to the council within six months and all works were to be finished within two years of the retention permission being granted.

Six months came and went, but no schedule of works was submitted by Cosgrave. Instead, he submitted a further retention application to increase the development to forty-four apartments. This was in turn refused by the council, and formal enforcement proceedings against Cavvies were commenced.

Cosgrave also took a case to the Residential Tenancies Board, for rent arrears, against the eleven tenants who had their HAP applications refused by South Dublin County Council. As a local TD, I worked with many of these families – first in an unsuccessful attempt to get their HAP payments approved, and then to assist them in moving out of the apartment block.

Thankfully, Cosgrave's case against his former tenants was unsuccessful; the Residential Tenancies Board determined that the developer's failure to comply with building control legislation meant that the landlord's claim to rent arrears could not apply, as the buildings were themselves not legal.

At the time of writing, the council's enforcement action is ongoing. Nevertheless, while the issue of building without planning permission and subsequently seeking retention is commonplace, Larkfield House is the first high-profile case of systematic and deliberate breach of the building regulations – a serious criminal offence, with the potential to land the guilty party with hefty fines and even imprisonment. Every single time Vincent Cosgrave allows one of his illegal apartments to be occupied, he is potentially committing an offence – each liable for a €10,000 fine and up to six months in prison.

Commenting on the case in the *Irish Examiner* in May 2019, Mick Clifford said that in the case of Larkfield House:

> The law was not so much broken, as completely trampled on. Regulations that were supposed to be watertight were exposed as little better than useless. And despite what has now emerged, there is, as of yet, no sign that any prosecution will take place.[1]

He went on to comment on the implications of the Larkfield House case for building control more generally:

> For the last five years, any time another example of shoddy and dangerous building practices from the

Celtic Tiger era has been exposed, the stock response from government has been that the past is a different country. Today, they point out, time and again, we have new regulations. We have sorted the problem.

The story of the redevelopment of Larkfield House suggests that very little has changed and that developers are still in charge of the law.[2]

Larkfield House is a test case. How this particular story ends will tell us a lot about whether Phil Hogan's 2014 building control reforms are indeed any better than the regime in place during the Celtic Tiger.

The apartment block is still occupied. When a property becomes vacant, ads are found on Daft.ie and advertised by letting agents such as Ray Cook. Rents are as high as €2,000 per month. Many of the occupants are in receipt of Homeless HAP, which means the state is paying for people to live in a building that is neither planning compliant nor building control compliant.

If this is allowed to continue, it sends a clear signal to every other rogue developer and builder in the country that building regulations can be ignored and developments can be built and tenanted – with the taxpayer picking up the tab.

I regularly receive complaints from tenants at Larkfield House regarding breaches of landlord obligations under the Residential Tenancies Acts. More recently, residents have been complaining about damp and mould. But fearful of ending up homeless, they are afraid to take their cases to the Residential Tenancies Board.

There is a need for South Dublin County Council to make a very clear and public example of Vincent Cosgrave and Cavvies. Too many lives have been lost and too much hardship caused for thousands of families because of defective buildings.

The fact that Larkfield House has been fully occupied since February 2018, despite its breaches of planning and building control regulation, should be evidence enough that our building control system needs further reform. The very least we can expect is that the developer is held to account for those breaches. If Cosgrave is allowed to get away with it, how many more Larkfield Houses will we have in the future?

The West Awakes

On Monday, 14 June 2021, between 5,000 and 10,000 people marched on Government Buildings. They had just come from a rally outside the Convention Centre, where the Dáil was temporarily sitting due to Covid-19 restrictions. It was the largest demonstration the city had seen since the start of the pandemic. The crowd was a sea of Donegal County jerseys, with a fair number of Mayo and Clare colours mixed through. Dublin jerseys were equally conspicuous.

Michael Doherty, a Donegal native and PRO for the Mica Action Group, described it as 'like travelling to Dublin for the All-Ireland football final'. As he and his family drove from his home in Culdaff, on Inishowen, through the neighbouring villages, huge crowds were gathering to get the pre-booked coaches. More than forty-five buses came from County Donegal alone.

But this was not All-Ireland final day. The people of the West of Ireland were not coming to challenge Dublin for the Sam Maguire cup. They were marching to demand that government provide 100 per cent redress for the thousands of homeowners whose properties were literally crumbling to the ground as a result of defective building blocks containing pyrite and mica.

Michael was one of those homeowners. A proud Donegal man, from a family of seven, he graduated as a mechanical engineer and went to work in Harland and Wolff. While living in County Down, he met the woman who would become his wife and they had their first two children. But his heart had never left his home county.

On his wedding day, his father, with tears in his eyes, handed Michael an envelope. It contained the deeds to Michael's grandmother's land in Culdaff. It was a large site, vacant for more than fifty years, with incredible views of the coast and surrounding countryside. There, in 2000, Michael would start to manage the building of what is now his family home.

In 2006 cracks started to appear in Michael's home. At first he thought these were just settling cracks, requiring minor repair works. However, over time he realised that the problem was more serious. Michael was just one of a growing number of people who were to discover that the blocks they built their homes with were defective.

In November 2014, 350 people attended a public meeting in Burt, County Donegal, all affected by crumbling building blocks. The meeting was called by the recently established Mica Action Group, who had been using an online survey and word of mouth to bring people together. Affected homeowner, and one of the founders of the Mica Action Group, Eileen Doherty, told TheJournal.ie, in an article published on the day of the meeting, that people had discovered a range of problems with the building blocks including the presence of Muscovite mica, which weakens the block when it comes into contact with water.

The homeowners were meeting with local TDs and the Donegal County Council Manager to see what could be done. The Mica Action Group wanted independent experts to assess their homes, and for government to establish a redress scheme similar to that provided for homeowners in Dublin and Leinster affected by pyrite in their foundations.

Eileen Doherty, Ann Owens and the Mica Action Group campaigned hard from 2014. All the while, more homeowners came forward. In response to parliamentary questions from local TDs, including Pádraig Mac Lochlainn of Sinn Féin on 27 May and Charlie McConalogue of Fianna Fáil on 17 June 2014, the then Minister for the Environment, Phil Hogan, repeated the line that 'building defects are matters for resolution between the contracting parties, i.e. the homeowner, the builder, the manufacturer, supplier, quarry owner and/or their respective insurers'.

When Hogan was replaced by Labour's Alan Kelly, the position remained the same. The new minister's suggestion, as reported by Inishowenindo.ie on 11 October 2014, that homeowners seek resolution in the courts, was greeted by widespread anger among affected homeowners.

However, there was some movement from government in 2015, when Minister of State Paudie Coffey informed the Dáil on 14 July that it was considering establishing an independent panel to examine the issue. The Mica Action Group welcomed the news, telling TheJournal.ie on 16 July that 'This is a very important step in the campaign for redress for affected homeowners … In setting up the panel, the government recognises the magnitude of the issue we are facing and it is comparable with the process offered to homeowners in Dublin, Kildare, Meath and Offaly whose homes were [affected by pyrite].'

On 2 February 2016, *The Irish Times* reported that the former Director of Services in Waterford County Council, Denis McCarthy, was being appointed by the Minister for Environment to head a panel of experts to investigate the issue of defective blocks and to report back to government with recommendations.

Unlike the Pyrite Panel established by Phil Hogan in 2012, whose report was published within six months, the expert panel on concrete blocks took sixteen months to complete their work. The 120-page document sought to establish the facts behind the emerging structural damage to homes in Counties Donegal and Mayo. Its findings were devastating.

The report estimated that somewhere between 1,200 and 4,800 homes in Donegal and 345 properties in Mayo had defective blocks. It expressed 'concern regarding the current level of enforcement of the Building Control Regulations and the Construction Products Regulation' recommending that 'these roles be strengthened significantly'. Most importantly the report concluded that 'the affected homeowners, through no fault of their own, are in a difficult position with very few, if any, realistic options available in order to obtain redress'. While the expert panel's terms of reference restricted it to establishing the facts of the issue, it was clear that a government redress scheme would be required.

Following the publication of the expert group report, the Mica Action Group in Donegal and a recently formed Pyrite Action Group in Mayo stepped up their campaigns. On 19 December 2017, the Mica Action Group met with Minister of State Damien English in Carndonagh. Eileen

Doherty told *RTÉ News* on the day of the meeting that the group sensed more of a commitment from government to find a solution to the issue.

It took a further five months before cabinet finally agreed, in principle, to a formal redress scheme for families affected by defective blocks in Donegal and Mayo. On 16 May 2018, Inishowennews.com reported that the scheme had been approved that Tuesday.

In response the Mica Action Group issued a detailed statement. They described it as a 'significant day' in which a redress scheme 'finally crossed the line'. While disappointed with the initial allocation of €20 million, they said they had 'been given an absolute assurance that this signals a genuine commitment from Government which will be evident through a significant increase in the budget year-on-year'.

In a significant section of their statement the group acknowledged:

> Some of you may be disappointed that a 10% per household charge will apply to the overall cost of repair/replacement of your home. We too in MAG are disappointed and frustrated. However, it is important to note that a NIL household charge would have required new underpinning legislation (as in the case of pyrite) which would have taken at the very least a year to bring to the statute book, and in our opinion may have put this very scheme at risk. Due to the very progressive nature of this issue, many homeowners simply do not have the luxury of time to wait.

The campaign had made a difficult but fully understandable call; in order to proceed with remediation, they had reluctantly accepted a scheme that provided less than 100 per cent redress. But their understanding was that this decision would result in the speedy establishment of the scheme.

Despite these reassurances from government, the final details of the scheme were not approved by cabinet until October 2018, followed by the signing into law of the Statutory Instrument underpinning the scheme by Minister for Housing Eoghan Murphy in February 2020. The defective block remediation schemes, to be administered by Donegal and Mayo County Councils, opened for applications in June 2020.

However, by November of that year the Mica Action Group were becoming increasingly concerned with deficiencies in the scheme. Following meetings with local politicians, correspondence was sent to the new Minister for Housing, Darragh O'Brien, setting out four issues.

The first was that homeowners would only be eligible for one grant. If that grant only covered the outer leaf of the building, they would not be eligible for additional support if further defects appeared in the internal structure at a later date.

The second was that, though the scheme was meant to cover 90 per cent of the cost of remediating the property, there were a number of caps and excluded costs, such as planning fees, internal fittings and temporary costs. In some cases this could leave the homeowner paying 30 per cent or more of the full cost.

There was also a concern that banks, who were ultimately benefiting from the scheme, were not providing any financial assistance to mortgage holders. Homeowners felt their mortgage lenders should contribute the 10 per cent cost, making the scheme effectively a 100 per cent redress for the owner.

Finally, a number of property types including rental properties and holiday homes were excluded from the scheme, which the Mica Action Group felt was unfair.

In February 2021, the Action Group met Minister O'Brien in Dublin to outline their concerns. That meeting was followed up with a detailed analysis of the first forty-three homes accepted into the scheme, submitted in writing to the Minister in April. This confirmed that the homeowners' contribution, even just for the rebuilding work, would be significantly higher than initially understood. The Mica Action Group estimated an average cost of €83,500 per household. The group was looking for an immediate review and revision of the scheme to address these problems.

There was also a requirement for homeowners seeking access to the scheme to pay upfront for an engineer's report, costing as much as €7,000. Though 90 per cent of this cost would be recouped if accepted into the scheme, this requirement was preventing many families from even applying.

As the Mica Action Group and their counterparts in Mayo worked tirelessly in the background to have the scheme improved, there was a growing anger among affected homeowners, their families and the wider community. With families in Counties Sligo and Clare also discovering defective blocks in their homes, the situation was quickly escalating.

After more than ten years living with defective homes, and eight years of hard campaigning for justice, the people of Donegal and Mayo had had enough. Despite the promises of a speedy resolution in 2018, three years had passed and not a single cent of redress funding had been drawn down.

When mica-affected homeowner Paddy Diver saw a delivery of building blocks to his neighbour from the very same company that supplied the blocks for his home, he finally broke. How could the company who supplied blocks to the thousands of now crumbling homes in Inishowen still be allowed to trade? Paddy decided to take action. He blocked the truck and posted the video of his stand on social media. The fuse paper was well and truly lit, the video went viral and a spontaneous protest movement exploded across the county.

On 22 May, Paddy, along with other mica-affected families, held a rally in Buncrana calling for 100 per cent redress. Thousands attended. With the public demand for justice for homeowners growing ever louder, a date was set for a march in Dublin.

Tuesday 15 June was one of the hottest days of the year. As the crowds began to assemble at the Convention Centre, the sun was bleaching the pavement. The mood was upbeat. People were angry but defiant. They had come in their thousands to send the government a very simple and very clear message – 100 per cent and nothing less.

Michael Doherty spoke for all those affected, not only from defective blocks, but all Celtic Tiger latent defects, when he told the assembled crowd that it was '100 per cent or shut up'. After the march he told me that people 'were not interested in anything less' that they must 'get justice'. He said, 'I will hang on the cross before I go back to accepting anything less than 100 per cent redress … we can do this the nice way or the hard way but we are not going away.'

On the day of the march, Sinn Féin tabled a Private Members Motion echoing the campaign call for 100 per cent redress. Deputies from every party and none spoke in favour of the motion and urged the government to act. In response Darragh O'Brien announced a time-limited six-week review of the scheme, during which everything would be on the table.

As this book goes to print that review is underway, as too are the deliberations of the working group on defective buildings looking at the wider Celtic Tiger defects issues. Will this government do right by the people of Donegal, Mayo, Dublin and elsewhere, and ensure 100 per cent redress for all homeowners with building defects they did not cause? Only time will tell. But as the people made clear on the streets of Dublin, anything less will not be tolerated and if the government falls short, the campaign for justice will continue.

Endnotes

Overture

1   Gareth Naughton, *The Irish Times*, 27.8.2014.
2   Minister of State Ciarán Cannon, Topical Issues Debate, Building Regulations, 23.11.2011.
3   Ibid.
4   Ronan McGreevy, *The Irish Times*, 4.9.2013.
5   *The Irish Times*, editorial, 15.10.2013.
6   Olivia Kelly, *The Irish Times*, 10.10.2013.
7   Ibid.
8   Ibid.
9   *The Irish Times*, editorial, 15.10.2013.

Chapter One

1   *The Irish Times*, 15.4.1999.
2   *Irish Independent*, 12.2.2016.
3   *The Irish Times*, 20.10.2005.
4   Ibid.

Chapter Two

1   Paul Melia, *Irish Independent*, 23.2.2010.
2   Thorntons Chartered Surveyors, Job Ref: 6925/EF, Property: Belmayne Defects Inspection, 2017.
3   Ibid.
4   Jack Horgan Jones, *The Irish Times*, 4.3.2019.
5   *The Irish Times*, 27.6.2006.
6   Ibid.
7   Ibid.
8   Ibid.
9   Louise Hogan, *Irish Independent*, 23.12.2009.
10 RTE.ie, 14.10.2011.
11 Omega Surveying Services, Fire Safety Issues, Galloping Green, PowerPoint, 12.12.2018.
12 RTE.ie, 22.2.2018.
13 Mick Clifford, *Irish Examiner*, 19.1.18.
14 RTE.ie, 22.2.2018.
15 Olivia Kelly, *The Irish Times*, 28.7.2017.

Chapter Three

1   *Irish Independent*, 22.9.2006.
2   CRO, Tudor Homes, B1 – Annual Return, 83454, 31 March 2018.
3   Ibid.
4   https://www.citizensinformation.ie/en/consumer_affairs/consumer_protection/consumer_complaints/where_to_complain_about_home_improvements.html.
5   CRO, Tudor Homes, Abridged Financial Statement for the year ending 31 March 2018.
6   Department of Housing, Planning and Local Government, Local Infrastructure Housing Activation Fund, Projections, March 2018.
7   Ibid.
8   Gordon Deegan, *Irish Independent*, 29.7.2009.
9   Clare FM, 27.10.2010.
10 Gordon Deegan, *The Irish Times*, 24.12.2010.
11 Gordon Deegan, *Irish Independent*, 29.7.2009.
12 Gordon Deegan, *Irish Examiner*, 13.7.2011.
13 CRO, Paddy Burke Builders Ltd, Company Printout, 125218.
14 *The Sunday Business Post*, 27.9.2008.
15 *The Sunday Business Post*, 6.5.2006.
16 Ian Keogh, *The Sunday Business Post*, 9.5.2009.
17 Ibid.
18 *The Irish Times*, 31.3.2009.
19 Ronald Quinlan, *Irish Independent*, 31.1.2010.
20 Bernice Harrison, *The Irish Times*, 8.2.2007.
21 Ibid.
22 Frank McDonald & Kathy Sheridan, *The Builders: How a Small Group of Property Developers Fuelled the Building Boom and Transformed Ireland* (London: Penguin 2008), p. 263.
23 Ibid., p. 265.
24 Laura Noonan, *Irish Independent*, 6.11.2009.
25 Colm Keena, *The Irish Times*, 13.4.2011.
26 Quoted in Mick Clifford, *Irish Examiner*, 5.7.2019.
27 Ibid.
28 Paul Melia, *Irish Independent*, 23.2.2012.
29 Jack Power, *The Irish Times*, 28.1.2019.
30 Mick Clifford, *Irish Examiner*, 5.7.2019.
31 Jack Horgan Jones, *The Irish Times*, 4.3.2019.
32 Self-certification refers to the process whereby developers certify that their own work is

built to appropriate standards rather than an independent inspection and certification regime, as exists in other jurisdictions.

33 http://print.cairnhomes.com/cairn-homes-plc-annual-report-2019/?page=10.

34 https://rebuildingireland.ie/news/contract-awarded-for-465-social-housing-units-under-bundle-2-of-ppp-programme/.

35 BBC NI Spotlight Broadcast, 25.2.2014.

36 Ibid.

37 Ibid.

38 *The Irish Times*, 27.6.2006.

39 Fiona Reddan, *The Irish Times*, 31.8.2010.

40 Seanad Debates, Thursday, 20 October 2011, Adjournment Matters, Priory Hall Development.

41 Olivia Kelly, *The Irish Times*, 11.11.2011.

42 Mary Carolan, *The Irish Times*, 17.11.2011.

43 Fiona Garland, *The Irish Times*, 16.12.2013.

44 Maeve Sheehan, *Irish Independent*, 18.1.2015.

45 Mary Carolan, *The Irish Times*, 1.6.2016.

46 Maeve Sheehan, *Irish Independent*, 18.1.2015.

47 Ciaran Barnes, *Sunday Life*, 19.12.2020.

Chapter Four

1 Paul Mooney, Owners' Management Companies, Clúid, 2019, p. 25.

2 Law Reform Commission, Report on Multi-Unit Developments (LRC 90-2008).

3 Clúid, 2019, p. 28.

4 Ibid., p. 28.

5 http://www.justice.ie/en/JELR/Pages/Ahern%20Launches%20New%20Deal%20for%20Apartment%20Owners%20Multi-Unit%20Developments%20Bill%202009%20outlines%20legal%20protections%20for%20existing%20and%20new%20complexes.

6 Ibid.

7 Ibid.

8 Clúid, 2009, p. 30.

9 Ibid., p. 32.

10 Joint Committee on Housing, Local Government and Heritage debate – Tuesday, 1 December 2020, Construction Defects: Discussion with Construction Defects Alliance, p. 7.

11 Ibid.

12 Ibid.

Chapter Five

1 http://www.irishstatutebook.ie/eli/2009/act/34/enacted/en/print#sec10.

2 Ibid.
3 *Irish Independent*, 20.6.2016.
4 *Irish Examiner*, 10.2.2018.
5 Ibid.
6 Ibid.
7 Parliamentary Question 50195/18 answered on 4.12.2018.
8 Minutes of the Shannon Municipal District Meeting, 20.3.2018.
9 *Irish Examiner*, 5.7.2019.
10 Ibid.
11 Olivia Kelly, *The Irish Times*, 10.10.2013.
12 Dáil Éireann debate – Wednesday, 23 November 2011, Topical Issue Debate, Building Regulations.
13 Ibid.
14 Ibid.

Chapter Six

1 RTÉ, Tragedy in Dublin as tenements collapse, 7.11.2019.
2 Ibid.
3 P3, Dublin Corporation, Report of Improvements Committee re proposed scheme for the clearance of the insanitary area bounded by Church Street etc., 1912.
4 James Curry, TheJournal.ie, 2.9.2013.
5 Padraic Kenna, *Housing Law, Rights and Policy* (Dublin: Clarus Press, 2011).

6 Dublin Corporation, Report of Committee on Housing [Part 94], 1914, p. 177.
7 Ibid., p. 180.
8 Kenna (2011), p. 35.
9 *The Irish Times*, 17.6.1963.
10 Ibid.
11 Kenna (2011), p. 44.
12 Dáil Éireann debate – 18.6.1963, Vol. 203, No. 8, Oral Questions, Dublin Dangerous Buildings.
13 Ibid.
14 Keane, 14.2.1981, p. 290.
15 *The Irish Times*, 18.8.1978.
16 *The Irish Times*, 5.5.1978.
17 Ibid.
18 Ibid.
19 The Law Reform Commission, Working Paper No. 1, 1977.
20 Ibid., p. 44.
21 Ibid., p. 45.
22 The Law Reform Commission, Report on Defective Premises, 1982.
23 Kenna (2011), p. 44.
24 https://www.thejournal.ie/ stardust-tee-up-2021-5276186-Jan2021/.
25 Justice Ronan Keane, Tribunal of Inquiry on the Fire at the Stardust, Artane, Dublin, p. 294.
26 Ibid., p. 312.
27 Ibid.
28 Ibid., p. 290.
29 Ibid., p. 312.
30 Ibid., p. 290.

31 Ibid., p. 313.
32 Memorandum for the Government, Report of Tribunal of Inquiry into fire at Stardust Club, Artane, Dublin 1.11.1983.
33 Ibid., Appendix 4, p. 2.
34 Justice Ronan Keane, Tribunal of Inquiry on the Fire at the Stardust, Artane, Dublin, p. 290.
35 Memorandum for the Government, Report of Tribunal of Inquiry into fire at Stardust Club, Artane, Dublin 1.11.1983, Appendix 4, p. 3.
36 Ibid.

Chapter Seven

1 Dáil Éireann debate – Wednesday, 28 March 1984, p. 1.
2 Ibid.
3 Ibid., p. 3.
4 Ibid., p. 4.
5 Ibid.
6 Ibid.
7 Ibid.
8 Ibid. p. 5.
9 Ibid.
10 Ibid., p. 10.
11 Ibid., p. 11.
12 Ibid., p. 9.
13 Ibid.
14 Ibid., p. 16.
15 Ibid., p. 18.
16 Ibid., pp. 20–1.

17 Ibid., p. 23.
18 Ibid., p. 24.
19 Ibid.
20 Ibid., p. 25.
21 Ibid., p. 28.
22 Ibid., p. 41.
23 Ibid.
24 Ibid., pp. 41–2.
25 Ibid., p. 42.
26 Ibid., p. 44.
27 Ibid., p. 44.
28 Ibid., p. 45.
29 Ibid., p. 46.
30 Dáil Éireann debate – Tuesday, 5 June 1984, Building Control Bill, 1984: Second Stage (Resumed), pp. 13–14.
31 Ibid., p. 20.
32 Ibid.
33 Dáil Éireann debate – Tuesday, 19 June 1984, Building Control Bill 1984: Second Stage (Resumed), p. 1.
34 Ibid., p. 5.
35 Ibid., p. 8.
36 Dáil Éireann debate – Wednesday, 15 February 1989, Building Control Bill 1984, Committee Stage (resumed), p. 7.
37 Ibid., p. 37.
38 Ibid., p. 9.
39 Ibid., p. 10.
40 Ibid., pp 15–21.
41 Dáil Éireann debate – Wednesday, 29 November 1989, Building Control Bill, 1984, Committee Stage (resumed), p. 14.

42 Ibid.
43 Ibid., p. 11.
44 Ibid., p. 18.
45 Ibid.
46 Ibid., p. 20.
47 Ibid., pp. 20–1.
48 Ibid., p. 23.
49 Frank McDonald, *The Irish Times*, 6.12.1991.
50 Ibid.
51 Ibid.

Chapter Eight

1   P.J. Drudy and M. Punch, *Out of Reach: Inequalities in the Irish Housing System* (Dublin: TASC 2004) p. 11.
2   Report of the Pyrite Panel, June 2012.
3   Ibid.
4   Ibid.
5   Management Company statement, March 2011, on www.arasnacluaine.com.
6   TheJournal.ie, 31.12.2015.
7   John Mulligan, *The Irish Times*, 6.6.2019.
8   Nina Buckley, submission to Joint Oireachtas Committee on Housing Planning and Local Government, May 2014, HPCLY-i-109.
9   Mick Clifford, *Irish Examiner*, 4.3.2016.
10 John Mulligan, *Irish Independent*, 12.4.2019.
11 Laura Noonan, *Independent*, 1.10.2009.
12 *Dublin Gazette*, 28.3.2013.
13 *Dublin Gazette*, 10.10.2013.
14 Millfield Hawthorns Concerned Residents, Submission to Joint Oireachtas Committee on Housing, Planning and Local Government, March 2017.
15 Mick Clifford, *Irish Examiner*, 28.8.2017.
16 Michael O'Farrell, *Irish Mail on Sunday*, 19.7.2015.
17 Ibid.
18 https://3ddesignbureau.com/news/1500-homes-planned-for-south-dublin-in-e375m-shd-by-victoria-homes/.
19 Barry J. Whyte, *Business Post*, 31.5.2020.
20 Sean Pollock, *Independent*, 31.5.2020.
21 Kitty Holland, *The Irish Times*, 20.3.2011.
22 South Dublin County Council, H-1(3) report to the Meeting of the Clondalkin Area Committee, 16.11.2011.
23 Dublin Mid West Sinn Féin, Balgaddy, a National scandal, February 2012.
24 Collective Complaint, FIDH v Ireland, July 2014.
25 Ian Begley, *Dublin Gazette*, 2.4.2015.
26 Resolution CM/ResChS(2018)1, 31.1.2018.
27 Ibid.
28 Kitty Holland, *The Irish Times*, 28.5.2019.

29 Ibid.
30 Kitty Holland, *The Irish Times*, 11.3.2021.
31 Niamh Towey and Jack Horgan Jones, *The Irish Times*, 4.3.2019.
32 Ibid.
33 Ibid.
34 Ibid.
35 *Dublin People*, 1.2.2017.
36 Niamh Towey, *The Irish Times*, 5.22.2019.
37 Ibid.
38 Jack Horgan-Jones and Niamh Towey, *The Irish Times*, 27.7.2020.
39 Ibid.
40 Department of Environment, Community and Local Government, Information Document No 1 to inform public consultation on the Review of S.I. No. 9 of 2014, April 2015.
41 David Reilly, TheJournal.ie, 4.4.2013.
42 Ibid.
43 Ibid.
44 Tom Reddy, *The Irish Times*, 21.11.2013.
45 Ibid.
46 Ibid.
47 Ibid.
48 Ibid.
49 Ibid.
50 Ibid.
51 Kevin Hollingsworth, *The Irish Times*, 27.2.2014.
52 Ibid.
53 Ibid.
54 Ibid.

Chapter Nine

1 CSO, Statistical Year Book 2020, new dwelling completions, Table 15.2, www.cso.ie.
2 Joint Committee on Housing, Planning and Local Government, *Safe as Houses? A Report on Building Standards, Building Control and Consumer Protection*, December 2017, p. 25.
3 Ibid.
4 Ibid., p. 26.
5 Ibid.
6 Ibid., p. 30.
7 Ibid.
8 Ibid., p. 53.
9 Ibid.
10 Ibid., p. 54.
11 Ibid., p. 55.
12 Ibid.
13 Ibid.
14 Ibid., p. 56.
15 Ibid., p. 74.
16 Ibid.
17 Ibid., p. 13.
18 Ibid.
19 Ibid., p. 15.
20 Ibid.
21 Eoin Ó Broin TD, 'Having the political will to prevent another Priory Hall', *The Irish Times*, 24.1.2018.

22 Letter from Owen P. Keegan, Chief Executive of Dublin City Council, to Eoin Ó Broin TD, 12.2.2018.

23 Ibid.

24 Ibid.

25 Ibid.

26 https://www.oireachtas.ie/en/debates/debate/dail/2018-05-24/26/.

27 Dáil Éireann debate – Wednesday 21 June 2017, Building Standards, Regulation and Homeowner Protection: Motion [Private Members].

28 Ibid.

29 Ibid.

30 Ibid.

31 Ibid.

32 www.constructiondefectsalliance.ie.

33 Ibid.

34 Joint Committee on Housing, Planning and Local Government debate – Thursday, 7 November 2019

35 Ibid.

36 Ibid.

37 Ibid.

38 Ibid.

39 Ibid.

40 Fianna Fáil, 'An Ireland for All', election manifesto 2020, p. 61.

41 Sinn Féin, 'Giving workers and families a break', election manifesto 2020, p. 68.

42 Green Party, 'Towards 2030 a decade of change', election manifesto 2020, p. 21.

43 Government of Ireland, 'Our Shared Future', p. 56.

44 Joint Committee on Housing, Heritage and Local Government, Tuesday 1 December 2020, Construction defects, discussion with Construction Defects Alliance.

45 Ibid.

46 Ibid.

Coda

1 Mick Clifford, *Irish Examiner*, 4.11.2019.

2 Ibid.

Index